The Customer Loyalty Loop

D0107220

The Customer Loyalty Loop

The Science Behind Creating Great Experiences and Lasting Impressions

By Noah Fleming

CAREER
PRESS

Wayne, NJ

THE CUSTOMER LOYALTY LOOP
EDITED BY PATRICIA KOT
TYPESET BY DIANA GHAZZAWI
Cover design by Howard Grossman/12E Design
Printed in the U.S.A.

To order this title, please call toll-free 1-800-CAREER-1 (NJ and Canada: 201-848-0310) to order using VISA or MasterCard, or for further information on books from Career Press.

The Career Press, Inc.
12 Parish Drive
Wayne, NJ 07470
www.careerpress.com

Library of Congress Cataloging-in-Publication Data
CIP Data Available Upon Request.

Acknowledgments

When you write a book, there are so many people on the sidelines cheering you on. As you get closer to the finish line, the cheering gets louder and more intense, the crowd roars, and then you cross the line. The first time I ran a half marathon, I felt like doing nothing for days. My feet ached because I embraced the then-popular idea of running barefoot. I realized shortly after the run that it wasn't such a great idea to try on the asphalt streets of downtown Toronto, and I paid for it for days. The point here is that there are so many people to thank during the process of writing a book and I can't thank you all individually, so consider this your collective high-five! Thank you all.

Of course, you have to thank your family. They're the ones who are there at the half-way mark with nourishment, brightly colored signs, and cheering the loudest—"Go, Daddy, Go!" Heather, Avalon, and Ella, thank you. I love you all so much.

Thank you to my clients who have worked with me over the past few years! Cheers to our continued success!

In particular, thanks to my agent, Esmond Harmsworth, who continues to support my work and ideas. And I can't forget my incredibly talented cousin, Holly Barimah, who designed the fantastic-looking process visuals inside the book.

And thanks to the fine folks at Career Press for believing in this concept.

Contents

Introduction

Let's get this out of the way, right up front. I'm not a psychologist or a scientist, and I don't play one on the Internet. Got it? Okay, good. Now that I've cleared the air, and you're still here, let's talk about what this book is all about.

This book is all about the work I do with my clients and how it can help you grow your organization, increase your revenus and profits, and keep your customers happily spending their money with you.

And while I don't have a PhD in consumer psychology, what I do have is an enormous interest in helping my clients to bring their customers back, to get their customer to buy again, and to persuade them to buy even more after that. That's what I'm good at; that's what my clients would tell you I'm good at—maybe even one of the best.

Now you could throw a stone in any city, click any random Internet link, and check your inbox on most mornings and you're almost guaranteed to find five "experts" promising to show you and your business how to get more new customers and close more business. The brutal reality is that not only is getting new customers fairly easy, it's often quite harmful if done incorrectly.

The truth of almost every business is that creating, nurturing, and ultimately profiting from a long-term relationship with your customers is much harder, but also that much more valuable, and the process starts long before your prospects ever talk to someone at your company. Most companies don't really understand what's required to keep a customer, and most certainly don't understand that something like customer retention and loyalty starts long before you have a customer in the first place. Consider, for example, a recent survey that found that 72 percent of small businesses planned to allocate the majority of their marketing budgets to customer acquisition efforts and only 23 percent to customer retention efforts. And of those, 30 percent of them believe their customers do business with them on a regular basis, but they're only guessing.[1] You can't make this stuff up! They're assuming their customers are coming back, but they don't actually know if it's true. This is the type of thing that surprises me. It shouldn't, but it still does.

That said, the research doesn't lie. And as I strongly argued in my first book, *Evergreen*,[2] most companies I talk to are spending the bulk of their time chasing new customers at the expense of building deeper and more profitable relationships with their existing customers. Why? Please tell me why, Master Yoda.

Okay.

Quite frankly, it's because it's more fun. It's sexier, and the feedback is near instantaneous. When you tell someone that they need to focus on their existing customers more, you're just telling them something they've heard a million times before. They've heard it at a million conferences. They've hired consultants and experts to speak at their organizations about servicing customers. They've read about it in dozens of other books. It must be important. Let's not forget the dusty, old chestnut that "it's five times more valuable to keep an existing customer than it is to get a new one!" The reason it's a big, dusty, old chestnut is that nobody has ever shown them how to make the existing customer five times more valuable. Don't you think that's a reasonable next question?

They've never been shown how to actually do the whole loyalty and retention thing in a systematic way that's measurable but also creates a demonstrable return on investment—something the folks in the C-Suite always need to see. Before I wrote *Evergreen*, there had never been a decent "retention" process to follow-up, maintain, nurture, and build relationships with our existing customers. Even the word *relationship* is one that's massively misunderstood in the business world. And in this book, I'm going to give you something even more powerful. While this book is certainly not a sequel to *Evergreen*, it builds on the fact that you've made the decision to focus more on maximizing the value of the clients and customers you've worked so hard to get. It's all about the mind-set. We can concentrate on new clients. We can concentrate on existing customers. Or, we can do both—right.

So let's get back to that psychology and science thing. What could a customer-retention guy possibly teach his readers and clients about human buying behavior and how to influence it—and more important, how the customer's experience has such huge implications as to if the likelihood that the customer will ever do business with your company again? Well, it turns out, quite a lot! Since 2005, I've worked with hundreds of companies and thousands of individuals. I've read and studied everything I could get my hands on from the conventional theories of sales and marketing to the modern pop-psychology books, and loads of insanely fascinating neuromarketing material.

But so what...that means nothing.

There are a lot of neat ideas out there, but not nearly enough of them provide pragmatic, useful information for when the rubber meets the road and the customer finally walks through your doors, visits your website, picks up the phone to call you, or finally pulls out her credit card and clicks "complete my order!" Yeah, just like all those other guys, I'll talk about the latest study and tell you why it's a neat insight, but what they don't show you—and I will—is how to actually use the stuff.

None of that other neat psychology stuff matters unless we understand how to actually apply it to our day-to-day efforts and the workings of your business, today. For me, my best source of learning has come from working with my clients and watching them in action. It's been about watching with a careful eye to see how the things we've put into place have worked (and sometimes not worked) and gauging the customer's response. It's been about watching the process of not just getting a customer, but understanding the importance of the entire experience every step of the way, and then paying careful attention to all the things we've done after business has been completed—to drive the customer back, or to generate referrals, or to create brand advocacy and positive word of mouth. These are all things that many of my clients practice and believe in because they've seen the results, and it's an area where so many other organizations need desperate help.

Some of the things I've written about in this book have happened by accident or perhaps, umm, backward! For example, if there's been an insight, a feeling, a moment, or a result where we've noticed something interesting, then quite often we've then gone looking for the science to back it up after the fact, and more often than not, we've found it. And after that, we've (*me*) has validated the learnings by applying them to the businesses of (*my*) various clients in different industries. Sometimes, we've found the science in peculiar places like the science of happiness or from psychologists engaged in bizarre activities like shocking dogs! So, what does this mean for you?

It means a lot. Most organizations become quickly entranced by this concept of "customers for life." It's a cliché phrase that's been used in various books and by dozens of speakers who then continue to give you the top 50 or top 100 things you need to be doing to keep the customer happy. In reality, most of them come up way short in providing systematic (and replicable) processes you can actually use to acquire customers and then keep them buying for a period of time, or allow you to continue to extract value for that customer. Thankfully, I'm actually going to show you how it's done.

Is Persuasion the Answer?

. . . .

There's also the age-old proverbial question, *How do you persuade someone to buy?*

More important, how do you persuade them to buy again, buy more, and buy more after that? You'll find the answer in this book. I'll show you exactly how it's done without driving your customers crazy. In fact, much of my work over the past 10 years has revolved around answering those very questions for each and every one of my clients. As mentioned earlier, customer loyalty starts long before the sale is ever made.

What about the whole word of mouth thing? How do we create "loyal" customers who spread the word about you? This book cuts through the all the fluff and gimmicks, and shows you how it's done in a simple, effective, and pragmatic way that you can actually implement. For example, I'll show you the fallacy of word of mouth. And no, I don't mean the negative word of mouth. I'll show you why even word of mouth that drives new customers through your door can sometimes be a very negative thing. That's just a few morsels of goodness we'll cover in the following pages.

The best news of all is this: It doesn't matter what type of business you're in; you can make these concepts work for your organization. My clients have ranged from small-town businesses doing a million or two a year in annual sales to commercial property developers with over a billion in assets to janitorial supply companies, to online and offline retailers, to extremely expensive business-to-business (B2B) equipment manufacturers, to small contractors, and so much more.

I've worked with companies offline and online, big and small, and just about everyone else in between. They say in the world of marketing that it's important to know your audience inside and out. I know mine—they have customers and want to learn better ways to engage those customers, to enhance those relationships, and to drive their revenue growth. They've spent time, energy, and money to get those customers in the first place, and they don't want to squander them away. The majority of my clients are mid-market, privately held companies with revenues ranging anywhere from $5 million to $1 billion in sales. Now if you're smaller than $5 million or larger than a billion, the good news is everything within this book is still applicable.

If you have a customer, then this book is for you.

Logic Makes People Think, but Their Emotions Make Them Act

If you've been in sales and marketing for any length of time, then you've likely heard that phrase before. It's an old phrase that has been repeated over and over again by the clever sales and marketing experts who have been carefully tapping into our emotions since the Mad Men age. But even some 40 years after Don Draper's Mad Men had people smoking because it might actually be considered healthy, we are still learning about why people say "yes," or why people finally decide to buy, and what causes someone to finally pen their signature to the dotted line. I help my clients with those concerns, of course. But the far more important question (in my opinion), and the far more misunderstood question is how to make it happen over and over and over again. And that's what I help my clients do.

In his classic book, *Influence: The Psychology of Persuasion*,[3] Dr. Robert Cialdini explained the psychology behind the reasons that people say "yes," or how to influence people to get them to say "yes." Cialdini is considered the seminal expert on influence and persuasion. The book, originally written for the academic world, sold poorly, but it quietly brewed for many years within circles of sales and marketing executives as the cult handbook of persuasion. It wasn't until almost 10 years after the book was released that it started selling like wildfire, raising Cialdini to a god-like status in the world of sales and marketing.

I had a chance to spend a few days with Cialdini, and even he was surprised by the book's late success. Frankly, even he couldn't really understand why it took so long to catch on and become a juggernaut of the business world, changing the way we interact with customers. One of my favorite aspects of Cialdini's work is that he claimed that the principles of influence were so powerful that they could be used for evil in business and that readers should promise to only use the concepts for good. Cialdini claimed you could have customers opening their wallets for you by tapping deep into the psychological mystery of the brain, or you could build cult followings and persuade people to do remarkable things by wielding this newly found power over them. Those are all catchy and sexy claims that get all the sneaky marketing folks sweaty and excited, so I'll make the same claim here.

The strategies and techniques found within this book are deadly. Used properly, you'll drive revenue and growth beyond your wildest dreams, but you have to promise me you won't use them for evil.... Promise, because they technically could be used for that. I'm just saying.... And if you do use this book for evil purposes, *definitely* don't use the material in Chapter 5! Now excuse me while I raise my pinky finger to my mouth like Dr. Evil.

With that said, it is time to get serious. Let's think back to Cialdini's seminal work for a moment. And by the way, if you haven't read *Influence* and you're in sales and marketing, it's almost impossible to take you seriously. I remember once saying this to a crowd of seasoned marketers, and many of them pulled out their phones and ordered the book on the spot!

But does the same psychology of influence that Cialdini taught us, which influences people to say "yes" the first time, also persuade them to continue to say "yes," again, and again, and again over time? Does the same science of persuasion make a person continue to do business with a company over and over again, or to become "loyal," or to become frequent and repeat customers? Are the principles of influence the same? It turns out they're not, and it turns out there's another set of principles that are an absolute necessity for long-term success.

Here's one for the highlighter and notes files: The biggest danger of getting a "yes" by using the tactics of Cialdini wrong is that you might not get the second "yes." Think about that for a minute. When it comes to marriage, most people typically want a single "yes." When it comes to getting your customers to buy from you, I don't want a single "yes." Do you? Of course not. Nobody wants a single "yes." The most expensive thing any of us in business do is get a customer. Do you want the customer to say "yes" one time or multiple times? Do you want that customer to tell others about the great experience they had with your company or go gently into the good night? The power of the Customer Loyalty Loop is about setting up all of your contacts, all of your marketing, all of your business processes, and your entire customer experience in a way that ensures people want to keep doing business with your company time and again.

Enter the Customer Loyalty Loop

The Customer Loyalty Loop deals with the psychology of customer experience, but more important, it's about understanding the psychology at each step of the client's journey and what you can do to influence the customer to continue to do business with you over and over again. I'll say it again: It doesn't matter what type of business you're in; if you have a customer, this book is for you.

Smart marketers have grasped the fact that they need to shift their thinking as it relates to the journey of the client. During the past 10 years, we've seen a demonstrable change in the marketing world generated from the collection of big data. This newfound marketing data has given organizations the ability to make decisions and create targeted and relevant marketing on a person-to-person basis unlike ever before. But has it helped us? Too many organizations are collecting loads of data but are unsure exactly what to do with it. Instead, I propose the collection of small data and the small insights that swing big doors.

In this book, I look at some concepts in behavioral science and psychology as they relate to the customer experience. More so, I draw connections to the experiences of my clients and the stories that have made me stop in my tracks and think, "there's got to be something more interesting going on here!"

At the end of the day, the goal is simple. I want to help companies better understand the minds of the customers through each step of the customer life cycle and, most important of all, to create a loop that keeps people coming back again, and again, and again—and telling others at the same time. Wait—not just telling others, but shouting from the rooftops.

You can tweak every step of your business and look for the minor areas of improvement that might increase profits slightly or create a small in bump conversion rates, or you can understand and control the customer's mind (not in the evil way, of course!) and create a cult-like obsession with your business.

In the early chapters of the book, we'll discuss the science and why the loyalty loop works as well as it does. You'll read the bulk of the "heavy" science over the next few pages.

After that, we'll delve deep into the Customer Loyalty Loop and then spend the rest of the pages in the book giving you the right tools to generate results. Throughout the book, you'll find various action steps, exercises, challenges, tools, questions, and workshops that will allow you to harness the power of the loop. Even if you pick just one area of focus, like Impactful and Meaningful Follow-Up, or The Psychology of Guarantees, it will have a drastic impact on your business. You'll learn from examples like Casper.com, where a single risk-reversal guarantee was the difference between selling a couple hundred mattresses per year and selling $75 million worth of them. It's not that they did anything special, it's just that they understand and embraced the various concepts of the Customer Loyalty Loop.

My clients often pay me $10,000 to $25,000 for a single day of speaking or workshops, and consulting engagements range from $30,000 to north of six figures. And they're always incredibly thrilled with the minimum 10-times return on investment. Many of the workshops and action steps found within this book have been derived from the work with my coaching and consulting clients.

What I have learned is that there are only a handful of things that can make any company, or any sales, marketing, and customer service department, infinitely more powerful. The companies tapping into these powerful concepts can be almost counted on a handful of hands and feet, but the principles themselves are more applicable and accessible than ever before. Let's get to it!

1. The Science of Experience

Marketers, perhaps more than others, know about the remarkable power of the story. After all, they are in the business of storytelling but, on the other hand, my story is very telling about business. While business knows about the power of the great story, it has neglected a critical part of the equation. And that's this: It's one thing to create an experience, but it's yet another to create a memorable experience. It turns out that a good experience isn't nearly enough. Marketing strategists typically have a good understanding that the experience is essential, but they have very little recognition of the fact that it's how those experiences are interpreted and remembered that is critical. There are a dozen books on the shelves all which claim to hold the keys to a remarkable customer experience! They say things like "wow" the customer by providing exceptional customer service, but that's only part of the equation.

To understand the core of the Customer Loyalty Loop that I'm going to outline in this book, you need to come on a brief journey with me into the mind. It's not complicated, and it probably won't be a surprise to you, but the implications of what I am about to tell you are pretty profound.

Human beings like to think they are rational, but very often they are not. While we have the capacity to be rational, the latest scientific research shows that by and large, we are more intuitive than rational. We make decisions more often with our hearts and minds than we do with our brains. There are a variety of reasons for this.

First, the brain's primary goal is survival and the first step in that process is recognizing threats. To function efficiently in this regard, we have to take what is going on around us and make sense of it—and to do that quickly. Without an understanding of what is happening, we can't anticipate threats or defend ourselves. So, we take in information through our senses and interpret it.

In other words, we create a story—and we do it very, very quickly, often without thinking. The idea or story just pops into our minds without any awareness of considered analysis. We, meaning *you* (who is reading this) and I, are customers, and we think this way. It apparently makes sense that your customers feel this way too.

Most of the time, the story we create is not based on a critical, reasoned analysis of the situation. Rather, it is an almost instantaneous, seemingly reflexive response to what we sense is happening all around us. Our stories are colored by many factors about which we are unaware. Subconscious experiences, intuition, instinctive reflexes, and the vast tapestry of our past experiences all quickly shape "the narrative" or our stories. The story quickly forms in our minds and for the most part, we accept it without too much, if any, analysis. Daniel Kahneman, the Israeli psychologist who perhaps has done more than anyone in articulating and explaining the relevant cognitive neuroscience research, calls this processing "fast and frugal." We create the story, and unless there is something that is obviously irrational about it, we accept it and move on. Kahneman, who won the Nobel Prize in Economics, brilliantly describes our mental process in his book *Thinking, Fast and Slow*.[1] He describes two ways of thinking based on two separate systems. System 1 is fast and frugal, as described above. System 2 requires critical, rational analysis.

Several biases influence the narratives we create. These are important factors that help us create those fast and frugal stories. Here's an example. Tell me, does this sound familiar?

> Normally this product sells for $99, but in this special offer you can buy this amazing product for just $39! That's a saving of $60! But wait! There's more! Order now and we will give you a second one free! That's a $200 value for just $39!

This is an example of what is called the anchoring bias. The first number (or fact) anchors the context to a specific point, in this case $99. Everything else is seen relative to that, so the offers do indeed sound like an awesome deal. Now, here's an important point. This tactic works even though most people understand that the initial number is likely to have been inflated! You have to make a concerted effort to override the bias. A vague awareness that the initial number is probably inflated isn't enough to counter its powerful effect. In other words, you have to make a very conscious effort not to be misled, and as we shall see shortly, most of the time we don't want to make that effort. We all know someone who has purchased the latest and greatest set of knives, the pan where absolutely nothing will stick to it, ever, or the latest and greatest piece of exercise equipment.

Another bias is the availability bias. This one means that if we can remember relevant examples, they will significantly influence our narrative. Here's an example. When there is a plane crash, and it's all over the news for days, many people will vow never to fly again. Or, they'll seriously consider alternative forms of travel. They do all this even though that as horrible as a plane crash is, that one plane crash hasn't significantly altered the safety of flying or the probability of being in an aircraft accident. If anything, that single crash is usually likely to make flying even safer. But because the accident is in the forefront of our minds due to the extensive media coverage, and the disaster is available to us, it significantly influences our perceptions of flying.

Now, here's a very critical point: It doesn't matter how accurate the remembered information is, it's the fact that we remember it that's important. Again, our thought process is not deep, critical analysis; it's fast and frugal. For example, you may have been hearing that coconut oil prevents dementia and cognitive decline. You have seen the research several times, so the repeated exposure makes it more available to you. Wow, so it must be true then, right? People rush to the stores and get a giant tub of coconut oil only to hardly ever use this stuff. I've got one in my kitchen.

However, if you take the time to do the critical analysis and look at the research, you'll find there is absolutely no scientific evidence for coconut oil as a preventive measure against cognitive decline. But who's got time to do the research on the research? It reminds me a lot of my father-in-law. One week he's eating eggs because the research shows the health benefits of eating eggs. Next week he's off them. New research shows how horribly unhealthy they are. Hardly anyone has the time or the skill set to do the research themselves.

It's much easier to go with what is available, that is, what we have seen in the media or what we think we saw in the media—and usually what's available at the present moment, hence the eggs. This availability bias will become critical later when we consider what factors influence the formation of memories, and how those memories influence decisions, including purchasing decisions, or the willingness to make a second purchase after the first one.

Another cognitive bias is risk aversion. Fear of loss is a powerful motivator, and most of us will overvalue risk because we're more afraid of getting hurt than anything else. It's a classic marketing hack known as "while stocks last" or "hurry, supplies are limited!" Some years ago, Beanie Babies were incredibly popular because the company making them was always implying that it was going to discontinue certain models. Amongst collectors, this fear of loss of missing out on one or more of the collection fueled the buying mania. You had to have them all.

There are numerous other biases. For example, I'm sure you have heard of the halo effect through which we exaggerate the qualities of someone we like by over-generalizing and assuming that they can do no wrong. Another bias is the social environment or what is called *social proof.* Dr. Cialdini argued that social proof was one of the six most powerful tools of influence. In a classic experiment, subjects had to say which of two lines was shorter than the other. It was relatively easy to see that line B was shorter than line A. But if you observe numerous people choosing line A rather than line B, there is a good chance you'll change your answer, even though B is indeed still fairly obviously the shorter line. What we see others doing influences our perceptions and our stories more than we care to admit.

All of these and many other biases serve the minds tendency to be "fast and frugal." We live in a complex world, so to minimize the effort of making sense of this complexity, people simplify wherever possible. This drive for simplicity is the default mechanism of the brain. As a result, the brain is binary, reducing the complexity of our world to simple either–or alternatives: right or wrong, Republican or Democrat, Conservative or Liberal (for my Canadian friends and family), and so on. As soon as we get away from the convenience and comfort of the binary brain, thinking becomes more difficult.

For example, what if someone proposed a three-party political system or even a four-party system? It's hard to wrap our heads around ideas when they are not presented as two opposites, or mutually exclusive choices.

The fact of the matter is that fast and frugal thinking is not only more natural, but it's also much, much easier. Critical, rational, logical thinking requires a lot of effort. Ask someone to do a mental arithmetic calculation while they are walking along, and they will almost certainly stop because rational thinking takes an inordinate amount of effort, and it's hard to walk and think critically at the same time. Even asking someone to do a small, less mentally exhausting task and the result is the same. For example, ask someone to text and drive, and you'll see why it's been proven to be almost more distracting than driving drunk. It seems every few days we hear about someone else who has walked into a fountain, fell down a manhole, or walked off a cliff while texting.

In fact, critical thinking is stressful, activating changes in the brain and body that are part of the physical stress response. Not only is critical thinking difficult, but most people aren't equipped in how to do it. Unless you have been trained in science and math, and even if you have been, the complexities of critical, rational thinking are likely to escape you. For example, Kahneman uses this great example in *Thinking, Fast and Slow.*

Fact #1: The lowest rates of kidney cancer occur in small, rural communities.

When you hear that statement, your mind will automatically go into a storytelling mode to make sense of the information you have just been given. Perhaps people in small rural communities eat healthier? Perhaps they have cleaner environments? Perhaps they are more active? Whatever factors you focus on, you will start to construct a story in your mind about why rural communities are healthier.

Here's the next piece of information.

Fact #2: The highest rates of kidney cancer occur in small, rural communities.

The natural reaction to this new fact is that there's a mistake and that the person giving you this information has contradicted himself. "That can't be!" you howl in protest.

You're wrong.

The answer to this particular problem is in the phrase "small, rural communities." In some small communities, there will be no kidney cancer, resulting in a very low/nonexistent rate. But if there's a couple of cases in a small community, the rate will be relatively high because it's a small community. In other words, this is a sampling problem. Small samples are going to produce a much wider range of probabilities because of the very fact that they are small.

Now, unless you have studied statistics, the idea of sample size probably hasn't occurred to you. Moreover, if you never got to hear the second fact, you would go on your merry way with the notion that small, rural communities are healthier firmly implanted in your memory. And that memory would then influence your behavior in the future. It would influence your discussions with others, and it would shape your worldview.

Now, while some simple arithmetic and math is not beyond most people, numbers aren't always what they might seem when viewed through the "fast and frugal" lens.

What's your first, instantaneous response to this question? You have to choose one.

I will promise to give you $3 million at the end of the month, or alternatively, I will give you one single penny today and double the amount every day for the next month, and give you everything at the end of the money.

Which would you choose?

Taking the latter option of starting with one cent and then doubling the amount every day will give you more than $10 million at the end of the month but "intuitively" that doesn't seem possible. In other words, rational analysis often results in answers that are counterintuitive.

There's something else that is critical in our storytelling; we need to be consistent. Our narratives, by and large, need to jive with each other. This drive for what is technically called *coherence* influences us in many ways. For one thing, we are always looking to reinforce and find proof for our stories. In the late 1950s, social psychologist Leon Festinger called this *cognitive dissonance*.[2] We have a selective perception that seeks to confirm our choices. So, for example, if you had to decide between car A and car B and recently bought car B, subsequently, you will find all the evidence that suggests car B is a great car and look for (and interpret) the evidence that shows car A's deficiencies. Today we call this tendency *confirmation bias*, where we overvalue information that supports our views and dismiss information or interpretations that run counter to our views. In other words, our narratives themselves are the lens through which we filter the world. What this means is that once you have a narrative about something, it is tough to change, or to quote the cliché, "you never get a second chance to make a first impression." This is a paramount part of the Customer Loyalty Loop, with one subtle difference.

The impression isn't the experience; it's the memory of the experience.

The cognitive neuroscience literature tells us that our perceptions and narratives are not based on rationality. Instead, they are significantly influenced by biases, including our existing stories, as well as a drive for simplicity. Subconscious memories and emotions also influence them.

There is some interesting research that shows that when people are asked to smile, they view (and remember) things more positively than when not smiling, even though the smile is forced. Emotions influence our perceptions and our stories, even when those emotions are artificially induced. The fact is that existing emotions color the experience and the memory of a situation or event. How would you react if you were just given a gift card immediately after learning that someone had been bad-mouthing you on social media? You'd almost certainly see the gift card as trivial and unimportant. Now how would you react if you got the same gift card after reading something flattering about you posted on social media? Chances are the gift card would be much more appreciated. In fact, you might even make a story about these two independent events. After getting the gift card and after reading the flattering social media piece you might think something like, "Wow, this is a great day! I'm getting a lot of love!" However, you might be so mad after reading the nasty social media post that it would be difficult to feel positive about anything, even the gift card, in which case you are likely to minimize it, or find a way of directing your anger toward it. For example, you might think the gift card is not appropriate, or the amount is too small, or it's too impersonal. You get the drift; emotions dictate the narrative even about things or events that have nothing to do with why you are feeling the emotion to begin with. In this case, the gift card could be a victim of being in the wrong place at the wrong time and is perceived through the emotion of the moment. And this, again, is because our response and thoughts tend to be fast and frugal and reflect our emotional states, rather than being a function of a rational mind.

These biases conspire to create not just our perceptions of an experience but our memories of it, too. The dynamic relationship between cognitive bias, emotion, and memory is a critical part of the Customer Loyalty Loop. More important, understanding that relationship is the key to improving your customer's experiences in ways that drive profits straight to the bottom line, and that's a narrative we should all be able to wrap our heads around.

The Memory of Experience
. . . .

Let's continue with a bit more of the science before we dive deeper into the loop. Elizabeth Loftus is a well-known, highly honored psychologist.[3] For the last 40-plus years, she has been researching something that is critical to each and every one of us, and a subject that has major implications for every aspect of your business, from marketing to customer service. Loftus is arguably the world's leading researcher in memory. But Loftus isn't someone who researches memory loss; rather, she investigates the process of remembering, which is critical to the Customer Loyalty Loop.

Loftus' research as well as that of others has highlighted something everyone could benefit from knowing: memory is unreliable. While most of us like to think that our memories are perfect recordings of events, the fact is that they not recordings of reality but highly individualized reconstructions that are subject to numerous sources of bias and distortion. As I have already mentioned, we invent our version of reality so it should be no surprise to learn that our memories are reflections of those stories, not a record of objective reality. Moreover, not only are those memories very individualized, but they can also be significantly altered by subsequent events. We'll talk about this in a bit when we discuss how imagination impacts our sales and marketing efforts.

In this chapter, I will examine the experience–memory–recall cycle. This is essential to the Customer Loyalty Loop. Companies spend a lot of money building their brand and creating a culture that supports a particular perception. However, that perception is going to be influenced by many factors, some of which are controllable by the organization and some of which are not. However, to give yourself the best shot at creating the impression, the brand, and the business you want, it is essential to understand the experience–memory–recall cycle.

Creating the Experience

The way we construct our stories, and our first memories of an experience, is a function of numerous factors. For example, we can only focus on one thing at a time, so when we focus to the left, we are missing what's happening on the right. And what's happening there might provide important clues that would influence the narrative. So, the first thing that shapes our story is where we focus our attention.

Once our attention is focused, we receive sensory input, mostly from the focus of attention but also from other strong stimuli that might be present. So, for example, as you're sitting at your desk focusing on the report you have to write, or as you're reading this book, you might be distracted by a loud noise, a strong smell, or even an unexpected vibration (those of you who live in places where there are earthquakes will know what I mean!). When distracted like this, the intrusive sensory input is likely to dominate your perception and subsequent narrative. It has got your attention for a reason; your brain thinks it's important as it is potentially a danger signal, and detecting danger is the brain's priority.

You're sitting at your desk writing an important report and doing very creative work. As you are doing this, you hear a deafening noise and looking out of your window you can see that there has been a major traffic accident right outside your window. What you will remember about this moment is almost certainly going to be the traffic accident and not the great work you were doing (but hopefully someone else will point out how talented you are!).

The human brain also works by focusing on contrast because contrast signifies change, and detecting change is a priority. As a result, the brain can be hijacked as it pursues contrast, sometimes at the expense of other important features in the environment. In their book

Sleights of Mind, neuroscientists Stephen L. Macknik and Susana Martinez-Conde recount their experiences learning magic tricks and illusions. They show that most of these tricks use the brain's natural mechanisms to fool us. The brain will fill in the gaps by creating illusions. For example, because the brain operates on contrast, if you show someone three red cards and one black one, the mind will focus on the black one first. If you withdraw the cards before there's time to look at the red ones, the illusionist has a pretty good idea which card has been remembered.

A classic example of how focus can influence perception is given by psychologist Dan Simons, as reported in the *American Psychologist* in 2006. In his talks, Simons performs the following trick. He has six playing cards projected onto the screen.[4] He asks a member of the audience to step forward. As Simons covers his eyes and turns away from the screen, he asks the audience member to select one of the six cards and point to it, so the audience knows which he has picked. In this case, let's assume it is the Queen of Clubs, but it could be any card. Dan then opens his eyes and says he will remove the selected card from the screen. With a click of the mouse, the screen changes, there are now only five cards left and, hey presto! The Queen of Clubs is no longer there!

How did Simons do it? Did he secretly sneak a peek when the card was being identified to the audience? Was it all a prearranged deal, and the audience member was part of the stunt? These are standard explanations that people give when they see this trick, but they are both wrong. In some ways, the answer is simpler than that.

No one notices that when Dan put five cards up on the screen after the audience has been alerted to the selected card, that they are five completely different cards from the original set! It's not just the Queen of Clubs that is missing, all of the original set are missing! Very few people notice, however, because they are all locked on to the Queen of Clubs and not focusing on the other cards. Our focus and expectations will determine our perception. There is a famous study on inattentional blindness featuring a flight simulation game. Professional pilots in this simulation were relatively weak at detecting when they were about to land their plane on top of another airliner! This is because it is not their common experience and expectation to see another plane in this situation, and they were focusing elsewhere. Many subconscious processes like these hijack our perception, experience, and ultimately our memories.

When we receive sensory information, we quickly interpret it with little if any focused analysis. Instead, our subconscious, past experiences, and expectations influence the story. For example, if I see smoke in the distance I might automatically assume that I smell burning as well. In that sense, the formation of our memories is based on associations and assumptions, of which we are not conscious, or at least conscious when they are occurring and influencing the story.

In the September 11, 2013, edition of *Scientific American*, Melanie Tannenbaum uses just such an example in her recollection of the events of 9/11.[5] Her recall of seeing the smoke from the Twin Towers from 30 miles away was always accompanied by the memory of the smell of burning. That was her enduring memory—until she looked at the numerous e-mails she wrote that day, not one of which had any mention of the smell of burning. It is an excellent example of how our memory fills in the gaps and uses unconscious assumptions that shape not just the narrative but the memory of it, too.

Now think about how this works at every level of customer interaction. If I see an ad that features a person who looks a lot like my brother, my perception of the ad will be influenced by memories and feelings associated with my brother (fortunately, in my case, mostly good!). Obviously, this can work in an almost infinite number of ways. Whenever you present people with a stimulus, they can react in many possible ways based on their experiences and associations. Sure, you can go out of your way to make the stimuli as pleasing as you want (for example, play soft music), but there are always going to be some people who react to that stimulus contrary to your expectations. For some people, soft music has negative connotations.

The Role of Emotion

Previously, I mentioned how emotion not only influences the narrative, but it also affects the memory of the story. The example I gave was receiving a gift card either immediately after discovering you had been bad-mouthed or praised in social media. The emotion not only influences the experience, but it also influences the memory of the experience. To give another example, you go to the movies with your friends to see a romantic comedy. Just before you walk into the movie theater, you have an upsetting phone call with your spouse/girlfriend/boyfriend. In the first scenario, you are in the movie theater and are distracted. You're thinking about the call and your relationship while your friends are laughing their heads off, which you find highly irritating. There's a decent chance that you will encode this experience as frustrating, and your memory is likely to be that the movie sucked as a comedy.

Now, back in the movie theater, let's suppose that hearing your friends cracking up makes you smile. Laughter is infectious, which is why sitcoms use laugh tracks. Now you are laughing, or at least smiling, and it is tough to laugh and be mad at the same time. So this laughter takes your mind off the relationship issue. Now, rather than underrating the movie, you're likely to overrate it! It must be a funny movie if it could distract you from your worries, right? But what about later when you recall this evening? The chances are that, regardless of how you felt at the time, if you now remember the association of the movie with the upsetting phone call, you will recall the movie as a disappointment.

In a relevant 2011 experiment, researchers showed that the more relaxed shoppers were, the more they were going to spend. Relaxation implies that the brain is not perceiving a threat, and therefore it is more capable of thinking abstractly about the value of the object and is less "defensive" about everything, including spending money. The defensiveness that stress brings might inhibit everything, including reaching for your credit card.[6]

As you experience events on a moment-to-moment basis, you are consciously but mostly subconsciously processing them. And after a few seconds, this experience is encoded into your memory. It's believed by the experts that the different sensory components of the experience—the sight, sound, feel, taste, smell, and the emotion—are encoded in different parts of the brain. When you recall the event, those separate memories are recruited and put together as a whole memory. Imagine having a separate file cabinet for each of these memory components. As you try to recall the event, subconsciously you go to each of the filing cabinets and collect the information needed. Of course, there's always the chance that you pick up the wrong file—a sensory impression that is similar, but belongs to another event.

If you have ever been traumatized or have watched or read about someone who has gone through a trauma, you will often hear that traumatized person be able to recall the difficult event but with no emotion whatsoever. In fact, they might say something like, "I remember it, but I am numb." This is because the emotional component of the memory has not been recruited, typically because it is too painful to bear. Sometimes the emotion is so overwhelming that it prevents the memory occurring at all, what is called *repression*. How memory is laid down in the brain makes subsequent recall susceptible to distortion.

So, now you have a memory of an experience in your short-term memory. At some point, it is put into long-term storage in a different part of the brain. Because it has been consolidated, you might think that this long-term memory; even though it has been influenced by the processes described above and is likely flawed, nevertheless will now remain stable. For better or for worse, this is how you will always remember this experience. But not so fast.

Remember Elizabeth Loftus, the memory researcher I referenced earlier in this chapter? She has been a leader in the field of how recall can be influenced long after the memory has been encoded as a long-term memory. If you had been a subject in one of Loftus' classic studies, you would have seen a picture of a car accident and then later asked questions about it. If you were in one group, you would have been asked to estimate the speed of the cars when they smashed into each other. If you were in another group, you would have been asked to determine the speed of the cars when they hit. The chances are that if you were told that the cars "smashed" into each other, your estimate of their speed would be higher than if you were told that they had hit each other. Moreover, if you were told that the cars had smashed into each other, you were much more likely to recall broken glass in the picture than if you were told that the cars had hit each other, even though no broken glass was present in the photo.

A lot of Loftus' work has been on this misinformation effect. How things are presented, the stories created, and the metaphors used all influence perception, subsequent memories, and more important, decision making. In a Stanford University experiment, researchers found that the metaphor used to describe the crime in a particular city influenced suggestions for how to deal with the problem. When the metaphor used for crime was to describe it as "a wild beast preying on the city," 75 percent of subjects suggested solutions that involve punishment and enforcement, like more prisons. When the metaphor was changed to a "virus infecting the city" only 56 percent suggested greater enforcement and 44 percent social reforms.

The misinformation effect also demonstrates that following information changes the reliability of memory. Loftus observed a murder trial where there was conflicting witness testimony, and after publishing an article about it, she became a sought-after legal expert who has testified in many high-profile legal cases, like the O.J. Simpson trial. What she has discovered is that various factors can distort the subsequent recall of memory. For example, the memory of witnesses can be significantly influenced by information they have got either at the time of recall or in the intervening periods since the event.

One aspect of this misinformation effect research has generated a lot of controversies and personal criticism of Loftus. In one study, in which the researchers created a false childhood memory of subjects being lost in a mall, 25 percent of subjects subsequently bought into the suggestion and recalled being lost in the mall as a real event that happened to them. Loftus then used this evidence to criticize certain forms of therapy, particularly where hypnotic techniques are used to retrieve memories. These techniques risk implanting false memories, especially of childhood abuse, Loftus argued. Interestingly, Sigmund Freud found himself in this predicament. Using fairly aggressive associative techniques, he believed that many of his patients were recalling experiences of childhood sexual abuse. However, when confronted with these "memories," these patients denied having any such experience. Were they in denial? Was there another explanation for the discrepancy? Freud resolved the matter by creating the notion of infantile sexuality, that children have a repressed desire to have sex with their parents, which in retrospect is probably the least likely explanation.

In any event, Loftus' contention that leading questions by therapists could create false memories led to howls of protests from therapists. Given what we know about the human brain and its binary nature, we should expect this argument to descend into a simple battle of opposites even amongst supposedly ultra-rational scientists (i.e., that there's no such thing as a false memory, or that all memories are false). Of course, what the research suggests is that memory is unreliable and can be influenced, not that it is always critically distorted.

And talking of the binary brain, there is some relevant research that relates to choice and buying decisions. One of the difficult tasks for the brain is to scale a list of alternatives. It is far easier to see the world as a choice between two opposites, than say a choice between several things that vary in different qualities. The binary brain might be behind the finding of one researcher on buying decisions.

Sheena Iyengar is the author of the book *The Art of Choosing*,[7] and in one of her experiments, she found that when subjects were presented with more than 20 types of chocolate or wine, compared to a list of fewer than seven, they consistently chose the premium varieties. Moreover, they paid considerably more than the product was worth. One explanation for these findings is that when faced with many alternatives, we're likely to simplify the choice by going to a binary solution and looking at the extremes. This would mean selecting either the most expensive or the cheapest. Moreover, we would overvalue those choices, making the "best" wines more expensive and the "worst" wines more affordable. Research of 63 wine auctions held in London between 2006 and 2009 confirmed this. People at these auctions overvalued the higher appraised wines and undervalued lower appraised products.

The nature of the binary brain, the focus on change and contrast, the influence of emotion, the way events are presented, our past experiences, subconscious processes, and expectations all not only shape the experience but also fundamentally influence the memory of the experience. And it is the memory of the experience that drives decisions. Also, each time a memory is recalled, it can be influenced by context and the availability of information that has assumed importance.

Melanie Tannenbaum, who was quoted earlier about her recall of 9/11, gives a great example of how subsequent input changes memories. She writes:

> John Adams and Thomas Jefferson both reported vivid memories at the ends of their lives where they recalled in graphic detail how wonderful it felt to sign the Declaration of Independence on July 4, 1776, the most momentous day of their lives. Except for one minor problem: July 4th was the day that the wording was approved by Congress. No one signed anything until August 2nd.

July 4, 1776, was obviously a very important date for Adams and Jefferson, and it had been so lauded after the event that even these signers of the Constitution forgot that it was not the day they signed the famous document. But you can see how easily that date would be part of their narratives and influence their memories of details. It's an example of the availability bias. The date of July 4th was so available to them because it was such a critical date that it influenced their memories.

Businesses go to great lengths to create the right customer experience, but what they should be doing is creating the right customer memory. And as you can see, there are many intervening variables that shape the memory from the experience.

The rest of this book deals primarily with how to create the "right customer memory." This starts long before the sale is made and continues as the customer continues to do business with you. To do this, let's start to unravel the various steps of the Customer Loyalty Loop so you can wrap your head around each step of the process.

2. Introducing the Customer Loyalty Loop

Now that we've covered some of the popular science about how memories are formed and experiences are remembered, it is time to dig deeper into the core of this book. Let's get down to brass tacks and discuss each stage of the Customer Loyalty Loop. More important, let's discuss how you can begin to put these principles to work in your business.

Succeeding at creating a memorable customer experience requires careful and meticulous attention paid to how each customer memory is created. For simplicity and to make this book as compelling and pragmatically useful as it can be, I've distilled the Customer Loyalty Loop into four distinct areas. Don't worry. I'm not going to use some random acronym, even though your mind is clearly designed in a way where if I were to give you an acronym like the word STICK or LOOP, even though you'd be far more likely to remember it. But that's fine, all you need to remember here are that there are four main steps.

If you think about the traditional customer lifecycle, marketers tell us that the customer follows a similar process. That process goes from awareness ("Hey, I just heard about this great product/service!"), to research ("This looks interesting, but does a better alternative exist?") to selection ("I've decided; I think I'll just go with this one."), to purchase ("Yes! I'll take the blue one."), to experience ("I love it!"), to retention ("Nice to hear from you again!"), to word of mouth ("You really need to try this!"). According to traditional sales and marketing, all customers follow this simple path.

There's nothing inherently wrong with the traditional lifecycle model, except each component of the model requires a complex set of understandings and skills, and most organizations focus almost exclusively on the first three or four elements of the traditional model. The majority of that effort is focused on creating awareness. Things like the customer experience, retention, and word of mouth are areas that are hard for organizations to understand and use to take meaningful action. If you want to experience all the benefits of the Customer Loyalty Loop, then you need to know what's happening at each step. The loop is a cumulative process, and at each stage you have an opportunity to either break or accelerate the process. Based on our previous reading, you've also seen how the mind can dramatically impact how the customer perceives the experience and what they remember. This is crucial if you want to improve the client experience and drive revenue growth at the same time.

The Customer Loyalty Loop is an updated view of the traditional customer lifecycle model, applied to the entire customer experience and the individual customers within it. It is a way of reframing the way that you look at your business to ask, "How can I make this experience better for an individual customer, and make it more likely that they'll want to keep doing business with us over and over again?" The Customer Loyalty Loop is about looking at the customer during each stage of the process and critically asking questions like, "How is the customer feeling right now?" and "What can we do at this step that's both remarkable and memorable to create a memory that sticks?" Let's introduce the four stages of the loop now.

The Four Stages of the Customer Loyalty Loop

There are four critical and straightforward stages of the Customer Loyalty Loop that we'll discuss in this book:

1. Imagination Before Persuasion
2. Conversion Without Coercion
3. Experience Choreography
4. Happily Ever After

It looks like this:

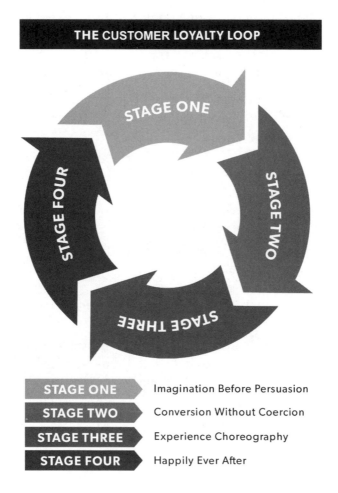

Figure 2.1: *The Customer Loyalty Loop*

Stage One: Imagination Before Persuasion

Careful attention must be paid to how the customer's experience starts. This might mean the first time a customer sees an advertisement. Or when a customer walks into a business for the first time. Or when a customer Googles a company's phone number to make a call and sees six customer reviews, or the first impression of an organization via an advertisement or word-of-mouth comment made by a friend. Marketing to a potential customer should be done in a way that carefully gets them to imagine all the great experiences to come and the memories they'll create. You must pay careful attention to the message you're putting into the marketplace from a very early stage. Instead of focusing on positioning, we'll concentrate on disrupting the mind of our potential customer to make our mark and increase our chances of making the first sale as simple as possible. This section is all about imagination and putting the right message out into the world to attract your ideal customers.

Stage Two: Conversion Without Coercion

In the second stage, we focus on actually getting the sale. Persuading someone to a point where they're ready to pull out their credit card, or sign the contract and do business with you, is completed in the second stage. Sometimes it doesn't take much work at all. The customer may just enter your business and be looking for something that you might already sell. And yet other times, we've only made it to this stage from our efforts to attract through sales and marketing efforts. In this section, we'll discuss traditional concepts of persuasion used to convert the prospect into a customer and introduce a far more powerful tool you can use to increase the likelihood of creating a more valuable customer.

Stage Three: Experience Choreography

This may be the most important stage of all, and it's certainly going to get the most attention in this book. In this stage, we begin the delivery of our core product or service. This is obviously going to be different for everyone. For example, you might be passing through a town and decide to choose a restaurant for lunch. In this example, stages 1 and 2 happen incredibly fast or perhaps not even really at all. The potential customer sees a place that looks decent, her spouse agrees, and they pull over for lunch. In this scenario, the customer walks in and is immediately thrust into the third stage of the loop. For others, like a traditional B2B firm selling high-priced manufacturing equipment or an enterprise software company, the customer experience starts the first time they hear about your product from outside sales, or at the first software demo or presentation. In that example, it is safe to say that stages 1 and 2 are far more important. And for others, like a hotel in New York City, the customer may move quickly through stages 1 and 2 on her own by doing their research. It's important to recognize, that in some cases, both stages 1 and 2 have been completed, and the third stage has begun before I've ever stepped foot in New York City. Even in that example, though, there are still things we can be doing to create the best-possible customer experience.

Knowing how to create, engineer, develop, and improve standard business operations and processes so that experiences are remembered is key. Everyone claims they offer a "wow" experience, but great companies have figured out not only how to offer impeccable customer service across the entire organization, but how to essentially manufacture the feeling of "wow."

But as we've discussed, it's not just enough to say you provide a "wow" experience anymore, because so do all your competitors! During the experience, you should be cognizant of the few big areas that people will take away (both good and bad) to form their memories, and develop a customer experience that ensures they remember the best version of their experience. For example, first impressions have never been more important. But what about happy endings? Understanding the importance of how your customer's experience ends is crucial to the lifecycle and profit potential of that customer. (This is also crucially important for the repeat customer, the lost customer, or the reactivation of that lost customer.)

At this stage, we also begin to battle the expectations gap. The gap is sometimes created because of overzealous sales and marketing approaches—promising something that is above and beyond what we're capable of delivering. During the past six years, much of the work I've done with organizations has been focused on the expectations gap and how we can close (or at least minimize) the gap.

Stage Four: Happily Ever After

The loop isn't a closed loop. It's more like a spiral. Our goal, remember, is to keep customers buying, buying more, and buying again after that. In this section, we'll explore some of the earlier science we've discussed to look at things like follow-up marketing and how to encourage word of mouth. We'll look at why post-service surveys are often a terrible idea and why most companies do them entirely wrong. In this section, you'll learn that all marketing to existing customers should be focused on reminding them of the best parts of their experience, so as to massage those memories into the most favorable versions. Why have people buy from you once when you can influence them and create an environment where customers want to buy again, and again, and again?

For most of my clients, getting a customer is the single most expensive thing they'll ever do. There's a massive amount of time, energy, and money invested in looking for ways to attract and persuade new customers to buy. Unfortunately, most companies forget all the other important things that happen after the sale. If they've closed the sale, the work is done. But the work is never done. In fact, if you only ever hear your sales and marketing people talking about "how to get a customer," then they're only doing half their jobs. Ask them if they'll work for half of their regular pay.

That's it. Four simple stages, all starting from long before the customer is ever a customer, to long after the first sale is made. It's not much more complicated than that. Some might quickly argue that the client's experience only happens in Stage Three and that everything else is unrelated, and that's entirely false. In today's connected world, the customer experience is the whole experience, and that's why it's important to understand what's happening in the mind of the customer at each and every stage and what you can do to ensure the best experience possible. It doesn't need to be complicated, though, and that's why it's important just to focus on four simple stages. Want me to make it even easier? Think of it this way: You have before the sale, the sale itself, the experience, and after the sale. That's it. Four simple stages with a few unique things you can be doing during each stage to ensure the experience is incredible.

Let's get started by looking at the first stage of the loop.

The Loyalty Loop Diagnostic
· ·

The very terms of customer service and customer satisfaction are entirely overused and really denote something other than what we're embracing with the Customer Loyalty Loop. Remember, the entire loop hinges on the fact that the customer has already begun to develop perceptions of you and your business long before they show up to complete the transaction. The customer is experiencing from the first time they hear about you in your marketing campaigns, long into your sales efforts, and long after the work is completed. For example, here's a small list of all the times the customer is having an experience with your company. Keep in mind, this is a list I'm rattling off one morning at 6 AM, and there are dozens of touch points and experiences that matter. But this is a good way to think about it.

1. The first time they see your marketing. Remember the awareness phase of the traditional customer journey.
2. The first time they hear about you from someone else (online reviews, friends, family, referrals, etc.)
3. The first time they call your business.
4. They first time they visit your website.
5. The first time they call you.
6. The first time a sales representative reaches out.
7. How your employees look.
8. The tone and personality of your employees.
9. The speed in which you respond to requests.
10. How you acknowledge problems or situations.

11. How you greet customers the moment they arrive and when they leave.
12. How you treat them during the experience.
13. How clean you leave the work area. There's a builder in the area where I live that leaves a huge mess all the time. It creates a really poor picture and impression in my mind of that builder. I'll never build a house with them. If they're cutting corners on cleanup, where else are they cutting corners?
14. Do you continue to follow-up after the sale, or do they never hear from you again?

As you can see, here are 14 things I've just rattled off. We're not even scratching the surface here, and the customer is continuously having an experience with your company. People love Disney because it understands the customer is continuously experiencing and its always looking to excel in every area. I remember reading a book once that talked about a white picket fence at Disney that's painted every night after the park closes. The paint dries just in time for the customer to arrive in the morning. Impressions are everything. The experience is everything. Customers don't remember decent customer service.

They don't even care if you deliver an experience that's just "good enough" across all four stages. The only thing that matters is that the experience is exceptional and that it shows that you've thought about it from before, during, and long after the sale. If you get the experience right across the entire loyalty loop, then you're likely to experience all of these benefits and more.

1. **Reduced sales and marketing costs.** When you embrace the loyalty loop, you increase the customers who are attracted to you. You won't spend as much to attract customers, because your customers can't stop talking about you. This increases your cash flow, your revenues, and your profits.

2. **Increased customer value.** The better the experience, the more consistent the follow-up, and the more you work to continuously add value, the more your customers will trust you. They'll spend more money with you, and likely more often. They're also far more likely to refer you to others.

The better the experience, the bigger the financial impact on your business. My goal in this book is to show you what that takes. To that end, I've created a simple the Loyalty Loop Diagnostic, a simple 38-part questionnaire to gauge how your experience measures up.

The Loyalty Loop Diagnostic is a simple tool for you to gauge how likely it is that your company is delivering a remarkable and memorable customer experience all the time. Take your time and carefully consider each question, and think about each question as it relates to the book. At the end, tally up your score and see where you stand. This should offer you some guidance on the areas where a few small changes or improvements would generate some fabulous results.

Action Step: The Loyalty Loop Diagnostic

1. Do you have a clearly defined, mapped-out, articulated process for what happens at each stage of the Customer Loyalty Loop?

   No (0), Somewhat (3), Partially (5)

2. Do you continue to market to your customers after the first sale?

   No (0), A little (3), Yes! (5)

3. Have you segmented your customer database between prospects and customers?

   No (0), Somewhat (1), Partially (3)

4. Do you have carefully segmented databases of both prospects and buyers to tell you at which stage of the Customer Loyalty Loop they're at, the last time they've purchased, what they purchased, the last time they spoke to someone at your company (touch point), or the last action they took.

   No (0), Somewhat (3), Yes to all (5)

5. Do you know who your top customers are by spending?

   No (0), Yes (2)

6. Can you tell me, unequivocally, the last time every current customer was spoken to and the nature of that discussion?

   No (0), Yes (2)

7. Do you know which customers are responsible for the most referrals or positive word of mouth generated?

   No (0), Yes (2)

8. Do you routinely communicate personally with customers?

   No (0), Yes (2)

9. Do you have a referral system in place?

   No (0), Yes (2)

10. Do you routinely solicit testimonials?

    No (0), Yes (2)

11. Does your business routinely receive unsolicited testimonials?

    No (0), Yes (2)

12. Does every piece of communication that leaves your office have a testimonial on it?

    No (0), Yes (2)

13. Are your phones answered promptly?

    No (0), Yes (2)

14. Do you return all incoming sales and service requests promptly?

    No idea (0), Within 7 days (1), Within 24 Hours (3), Within 90 minutes (6)

15. Do you know where every incoming lead goes and if it's followed up on?

    No (0), A little (1), Yes (2)

16. Do you know that every time you provide a quote or a proposal the quote is followed up on?

    No (0), I think so (1), Yes (2)

17. Do you know your current attrition rate?

    No (0), Yes (2)

18. Do you know why customers stop doing business with you?

    No (0), Yes (2)

19. Do you engage in regular customer reactivation campaigns?

    No (0), Yes (2)

20. Have you carefully articulated your customer archetypes?

    No (0), Yes (2)

21. Do you know how much a customer is worth to your business and what you're willing to spend to get one?

No (0), Yes (2)

22. Do you use guarantees and risk reversals?

No (0), Yes (2)

23. Do you employ recurring revenue models or subscription-based offerings?

No (0), Yes (2)

24. Are you constantly looking for new ways to improve your customer service?

No (0), Yes (2)

25. How often do you send regular, nonpromotional materials to your prospects and customers?

Rarely (0), Quarterly (2), Monthly (4), Weekly (5)

26. How often are you creating new content for your website?

Rarely (0), Quarterly (2), Monthly (4), Weekly (5)

27. Do you perk, reward, and create special events, or exclusive product and service offerings only for your top customers?

No (0), Yes (2)

28. Do you routinely shop your competition?

No (0), Yes (2)

29. Have you created your own Remarkable Moments?

No (0), Yes (2)

30. Do you use NPS scoring as your main source of customer feedback?

Yes (0), No (2)

31. Do you understand the buying cycle of your customers and know when they should be buying from you again?

No (0), Yes (2)

32. Do you market to customers who should be buying, accordingly, at the right time?

No (0), Yes (2)

33. Do your employees have the authority to make an unhappy customer happy within reason? (This means, they can spend money—again, within reason—to fix a

situation without managerial approval, and they know exactly how much they can spend to fix it.)

No (0), I think so (1), Yes, within reason (2), We have a specific amount an employee can spend to fix the situation without any need for approval (4)

34. Is every employee able to answer basic questions about your business? (Where are the restrooms? Where is the front desk? Who can help me with X? Who do I need to speak to to get something fixed?) If tested on this, would every employee pass with flying colors?

No (0), Maybe (1), Unequivocally (4)

35. Does the CEO or president (perhaps that is you?) of the company work on the front lines and directly with customers at least once every 90 days?

No (0), Yes (2)

36. If I asked all your individual sales representatives to map out and define your entire sales process, they would all be the same?

No (0), Yes (2)

37. Do you understand the top five causes of resistance and skepticism of your prospects in Stage Two?

No (0), Yes (2)

38. Do you use the Cialdini principles of influence, even if they're not entirely true (e.g., scarcity)?

No (2), Yes (0)

100 total score ____

The Answer Key

The next step is to tally up your scores and see how you rank.

A) **If your total points are 51 or less,** it tells you that you're likely delivering a very poor customer experience. Your business could be stable, profitable, and seem to be doing well, but your greatest opportunity for growth revolves around creating a well-balanced, cohesive customer experience by understanding each stage of the loyalty loop. You're likely losing customers regularly and investing a ton of time, money, and energy into customer acquisition efforts.

B) **If your total points are between 52 and 89,** you're delivering a decent customer experience. You have an understanding of each stage of the customer experience, but small hinges will swing big doors. You have room for exceptional improvements. You can likely improve profits and revenue by 50–60 percent or more by working on a small number of the things you're not doing.

C) **If your total points exceed 90 or higher,** congrats! I'm willing to guess you're delivering a wonderful customer experience and your business results are confirming that. However, even though you've ranked so high, this creates even more opportunity to tweak, improve, and create dramatic growth opportunities by harnessing the power of the loyalty loop. Regardless, you deserve a high-five for a job well done. Now keep improving, keep tweaking, and keep testing. Utilize the action steps found here to embrace continuous improvement. The test is designed such that a perfect score *is* possible—can you get there?

3. Stage One: Imagination Before Persuasion

"MEN WANTED for Hazardous Journey. Small wages, bitter cold, long months of complete darkness, constant danger, safe return doubtful. Honour and recognition in case of success." —*Ernest Shackleton, 4 Burlington Street*

As the story goes, this ad was placed in London newspapers in the early 1900s. The story claimed that the ad generated at least 5,000 responses from men and women of all ages ready to embark on the adventure of a lifetime. The ad's response was a catalyst for claiming its spot in a book titled *The 100 Greatest Advertisements of All Time*.[1] The ad was supposedly written by an Arctic explorer named Ernest Shackleton. Unfortunately, the ad might be a myth. It may have never even been published. One website has devoted the past 15 years to trying to find a copy of the advertisement and put up a $100 cash bounty for anyone who can find it.[2] Dozens of Internet sleuths have searched the microfiche archives of hundreds of newspapers and nobody has yet to locate it. I'd suggest increasing the bounty, but we'll come back to this ad shortly.

Sales, marketing, and loyalty experts are continuously talking about the traditional customer journey. We've already spoken about this in the previous section. All too often, those experts view the first two or three parts of the traditional customer lifecycle as the most important, but then fail to focus enough (and sometimes any) attention on the additional steps (and perhaps the most important steps in helping us maximize profits and revenue for our organizations).

Talented marketers, expert copywriters, salespeople, user-experience wizards, growth hackers, and so on almost all exclusively focus the majority of their efforts on taking from the customer from a point of interest, to getting the customer to hand over a bundle of cash. If they've reached that point, then the job is complete. And as I continue harping at you, the job is never complete!

We've all heard the dusty, old chestnut that it cost as much as 5 times more to acquire a new customer than it does to keep an existing one. One of the problems with presenting new and existing customers this way is that it undervalues the process of trying to keep an existing customer. Making it a binary brain issue—new customers vs. existing ones—and showing how much it takes to get the new customer is likely to result in actually minimizing the customer retention effort. However, an existing customer is a new customer; these two categories are a false division because they are not alternatives—they are the same person, just at a different stage of the process! It's a bit like a medical practice putting all of its efforts into diagnosing people and hardly any into treating them. Another problem with the false division between new and existing customers, and in particular the statement that it costs 5 times as much to acquire a customer as it does to keep them, is that nobody ever tells us how to make the existing customer 5 times more profitable. But I did. And not to toot my own horn, but this was covered in great detail in my previous book, *Evergreen*. There I espoused not just a strategic framework that would allow companies to understand better who they are, who they're doing it for, and how to nurture and cultivate deeper, more meaningful, and more profitable customer relationships, but the main point was really about creating a mind-set shift. This mind-set shift focused on the fact that companies are spending enormous amounts of time, energy, and resources on hunting for new business as opposed to caring for and nurturing the customer from the point of the first contact to a long and fruitful life doing business with your company.

To take things to the next level, it begins with the Customer Loyalty Loop and understanding the psychology of the new customer experience.

Customer Archetypes

Throughout the book, we talk about why tactical persuasion tactics will only get us so far. If you want to succeed in Stage One of the loyalty loop, there is nothing more important than truly understanding who your buyers are so that you can create marketing and messaging that speaks to them directly. In Stage Two, you need to know their wants, fears, and desires so you can properly remove resistance from the sale. In Stage Three, it's incredibly important to make the actual customer experience as personal and meaningful as you can. It's a bit of a fun exercise, but it's incredibly telling. I've done this exercise with executive teams, CEOs, and sales and marketing people. Almost always, we find that people know more about the people they watch on television after work than the people they are charged with serving on a daily basis. If you want to master the loyalty loop, it's incredibly important to know your ideal customer inside and out.

At my recent Evergreen Summit, I asked a group of executives to explain, in detail, a favorite TV character. At first, they looked at me in bewilderment, but then they took part. For two minutes, heads were down as people crafted incredibly detailed descriptions of Walter White from *Breaking Bad*, Larry David from *Curb Your Enthusiasm*, Charlie from *Two and a Half Men*, and others. I asked someone to share what they had written, and a highly successful CEO went on to explain Walter White in incredible detail. He told where he worked, what kind of car he drove, what color hair he had, what his struggles were, what his family was like, and so on. The list went on and on. Others in the room also wrote incredibly detailed narratives describing their favorite characters. When they were done, I asked the group to flip over their paper and write a detailed narrative of their ideal customer. The participants got down to work, but I could see instantly this was a lot harder than it looked. Finally, one attendee blurted out, "Okay, Noah! Point taken!" Everyone laughed, but nearly everyone agreed that it was much easier to write a description of our favorite TV character than writing a description of our ideal customers. But why is that? It should be the other way around. This is a fabulous exercise to do with both your sales, marketing, and customer-facing employees.

Action Step: The Walter White Workshop

Step 1: Ask your team to write detailed descriptions of their favorite television or movie characters. Give everyone about five minutes to complete the exercise.

Step 2: Spend a few minutes allowing people to share. Make note of all the small, yet important details they know about the fictional character.

Step 3: Ask them to complete the exercise creating a detailed description of your ideal customer. This is important to do across teams and various departments.

Step 4: If you find wildly different descriptions of your ideal customers, then you'll need to work together to craft your buyer personas.

If it were evident that your people need a lot of help in this area, then I would urge you to spend time learning more about your customer archetypes. If you found that your people genuinely have a good idea of who your customers are and what's important to them, then go ahead and skip to the next exercise. There is nothing more valuable than a comprehensive, thorough, deeply psychological and emotional understanding of your entire customer base. You need to understand how to reach each type of customer, what resonates with them, and how to speak to them. You can only find the ones you want if you know what you're looking for. The Walter White exercise is a great way to see if your people truly understand the customers they are serving. It's important to the entire experience as it guides people on how to effectively communicate with your customers.

Meaningful, Memorable, and Personal

One of the underlying assumptions of all great customer service delivery and exceeding customer's expectations is to understand the power of personalization in a world gone mad with automation and cost-cutting, and how to balance that personalization with the automation of the right elements of your business to maximize the impact of that personal touch. The customer experience must be meaningful, memorable, and personal. Too many companies drop the ball when it comes to providing experiences that are personalized, positive, and consistent. Today more than ever, larger organizations are tapping into large amounts of data to provide these more "individualized" experiences. All companies of all sizes need to recognize the power of ensuring that experiences are personalized, positive, and consistent. Even something as simple as sending a letter to a longtime customer that reads, "Dear Valued Customer," can create feelings of resentment with that longstanding customer. Is the customer truly valued? Was your call really important to them? Organizations need to be mindful of how the experience starts and how the experience ends as two key opportunities to influence the mind of a new customer and one that becomes a loyal customer.

Are there easy ways to increase customer satisfaction? According to research, there are. In a study done with waiters at a restaurant, they were able to significantly increase their tips, showing that customers felt better about the service, through a very simple strategy. The waiters would bring table mints and, some time later, they would come by the table again and offer more mints, in case the people at the table wanted more. This alone increased tipping by 23 percent.

What does this study show us? It suggests that offering a more personalized and careful attention to the customers, even when this is expressed through small things like offering more mints, can significantly increase customer satisfaction.

There are a couple of ways in which the study is relevant for the Customer Loyalty Loop. First, it shows that small details, such as free bonuses, personalized attention, and follow-ups, among other things, can significantly increase customer satisfaction, increasing their loyalty as well. Second, it shows the importance of showing concern for the customer's needs in a noninvasive manner. In this case, the waiter came to offer more mints because he wondered if the table needed more. For the customer, that shows that the waiter took them into consideration and showed some concern for their needs, making the service that they received far more personal, even if it was only done at the end of the meal.

In general, this study suggests that by showing concern for and attention to the customer even through small details, customer service can be significantly improved, raising customer loyalty and satisfaction. For example, after someone buys, consider calling them to thank them. Simple. Don't forget the power of handwritten notes. Hardly anyone is using it, and it always generates a wonderful response.

Action Step: Touch Points Workshop

Look at all the little customer touch points throughout the entire loyalty loop and brainstorm ways you can make each part of the process more meaningful, memorable, and personal.

If someone books a stay at your hotel, instead of e-mailing them a confirmation letter, call them to follow up. If someone has purchased something from you, or you've installed something at their place of business, stop by every once and a while and check it out.

Finally, depending on what type of business you're in, categorize your clients even further. Make note of their interests personally and professionally. Here's what I mean. For me, it's simple; I usually take on about six to eight large projects a year, keeping my client base relatively small at any one time. I have a number of coaching, mentoring, and speaking clients, but the larger projects I'm engaged in are manageable to the point I know a lot about each one of their businesses. I'll routinely capture and maintain articles, stories, and things I find that might be of interest to that client. I'll maintain a file and send them once a month. I'm not suggesting everyone gets something monthly, but if I have a client in the funeral industry and see an interesting piece of content in the *New York Times* on that specific industry, I'll clip the article and/or forward it with a brief, personal note. "Shawn, this is interesting as it related to the work we're doing with your sales team. What are your thoughts?"

It's meaningful, memorable, and personal. There's nothing malicious about this; it's pure added value. It might be impossible to scale this to hundreds or thousands or millions of customers, but it doesn't need to be. I have another client who has a keen interest in fishing—so do I. I'm constantly sending him interesting things I see, and he appreciates it.

Think about what you'd like your customers to be saying about your business.

Workshop: Take a Compliment

Get your team together and brainstorm on the following questions.

- What are the three to five best compliments and words of praise a customer can give your business?
- Are you doing enough to influence those compliments and words of praise?
- Are current reviews and testimonials confirming that you're getting those compliments?
- If you're not, where else do you need to improve? What can and should you be doing to ensure you're getting those compliments and words of praise?

The New Customer Experience
· ·

In the first stage, we start with the beginnings—before the sale. This is the first time the customer is exposed to your brand or the moment the idea of your company is first planted in their head. This is counterintuitive for many, but the Customer Loyalty Loop starts long before the sale has ever been made. It starts from the very first time a prospect is exposed to your sales, marketing, and advertising efforts. It's that first time they read an ad in a London newspaper that stops them completely in their tracks and makes them say, "Sign me up for that adventure!" It's the first time they open their mailbox to find a brochure from your firm. It's the first time they find you via a Google search. It's the first time they're told by a trusted colleague that they need to implement your enterprise software solution or your sales approach. The impressions and the memories of these initial encounters with your product are the platforms on which all subsequent actions are based. This stage becomes all about the behavior of the customer, understanding how our actions align with how they're feeling, and more important, how they're making decisions. We begin by asking ourselves questions like, "How can I better understand what is happening at this point, and how can I use that information to improve my sales and marketing efforts?"

In Stage One, the real secret is about learning how to tell your story in a way that implants a positive movie into the potential customer's head and makes them want to maintain their interest in you and ultimately do business with your company.

There are some ways we can accomplish this proactively, and we'll discuss a few of them. Also, I'll discuss the science behind why this works and provide action steps so you can look at your efforts at this stage and make immediate improvements.

One of the ways we can accomplish this is through a concept called preemptive marketing.

Preemptive Marketing

One of the greatest marketing breakthroughs of our time came from a strategist by the name of Claude Hopkins.[3] Here are two crazy things you might not know about this: One, this sales and marketing breakthrough occurred back in 1919, and two, it's hardly ever used today, even though it's more relevant than ever with the rise of social media and new tools for digital storytelling. It's one of the most powerful marketing techniques you could ever employ. Further to that, it's crucial in the first stage of the loyalty loop. Here's the story.

The Schlitz beer company needed help. In the late 1800s, Schlitz became known as the beer that put Milwaukee on the map, but after the turn of the century, the sales for Schlitz began to drop. They were getting crushed and losing market share in an increasingly competitive marketplace. They felt that they had a fantastic product, but it was becoming harder and harder to compete because everyone was selling the same product. The product became commoditized, or so they assumed, but they knew they needed help, so they took the plunge and hired a fantastic consultant by the name of Claude Hopkins. A quick note of shameless self-promotion here: it's important to hire great consultants. (Like me!)

Hopkins was the Don Draper of his time. He traveled to the Schlitz factory to meet the executives and toured the facilities. As the executives took him on what was probably a pretty standard tour of the brewing facility, Hopkins was amazed at everything he saw. For example, he noted that the factory sat on the edge of one of the Great Lakes, where water flowed into four large basins, feeding the plant with an endless supply of clean water. As the tour continued, he was shocked at the love and care that went into producing what had seemingly become an undifferentiated commodity. Schlitz, for example, showed Hopkins its research center where the company was performing thousands of experiments on yeasts to perfect the quality and purity of the final product. He saw the bottle-cleaning area, where bottles were washed a minimum of 12 times to remove all the impurities from the bottle, resulting in the best-quality beer they could produce. He noted that many of the scientific testing areas were encased in glass with air purification filters and workers adorned with lab coats. All of this was done to protect the product from impurities getting into the beer. When Hopkins finished the tour, he was stunned and asked the executives, "Why aren't you telling your customers about this?" And they responded, "Because all beer is made this way." Hopkins thought for a moment and said, "You're right, but nobody is telling the public about this."

Almost every product and service is a commodity to an extent. There's very little differentiation between most products and services. In fact, most companies sell products that are very close in quality, at similar prices, to a similar audience, using similar advertising. In a nutshell, companies do struggle to differentiate themselves.

Hopkins recognized the power of telling your story before anyone else could in a way that stoked a fire inside your prospect's mind. Jay Abraham, one of the greatest marketing experts of our time, has called this the concept of preemptive marketing.[4] Preemptive marketing is about everything that happens before the sale—the ability to implant a story in the customer's mind, before persuading them to buy. While most companies are waiting for prospects who are ready to buy, preemptive marketing is about building the trust, the relationship, and story long before your competitors have even had a chance to influence the potential customer. This creates an unfair competitive advantage, and it's available for you to use right now. Hopkins went on to create messaging for Schlitz around the concept of purity. Every beer manufacturer was calling their beer pure. But what Hopkins did was different. What he did was explain why and how the beer was pure. For example, one ad explained that the Schlitz's brown bottle provided an extra level of security against sunlight, which would spoil beer in lighter bottles. Were others using brown bottles? Sure, but nobody else was explaining why. Another ad urged consumers to ask their doctor about the purity of Schlitz beer—because "He knows the importance of purity."[5]

What does science tell us about preemptive marketing, and why does it work? Is there any research to back up why preemptive marketing has an impact? For this, we look to the work of one of my favorite social psychologists and his work on happiness. A Harvard social psychologist and author of the book *Stumbling on Happiness*,[6] Dan Gilbert provides us with an interesting insight as to why this works, the way it does, and how we can further take advantage of preemptive marketing. Gilbert says that "people believe everything they read or hear—whether truth, fiction, or outright lie—when they first read it or hear it. It is only afterward they may come to disbelieve it." In a nutshell, people believe everything at least for a second. Preemptive marketing allows you to be first to plant a story in the customer's mind, and it's a powerful concept we can all use. That's not to say we're planting truth, fiction, or outright lies, but we can be in charge of telling our story and ensuring it's the one that differentiates us from our competitors. More so, the repeated use of those stories makes everything even more believable.

Think of the concept of preemptive marketing as your opportunity to plant the seed of imagination and a memory inside your prospective customer's head before your competitors even have a chance at getting their attention. Too many branding, advertising, and marketing companies are obsessed with trying to get some moment of awareness through all that noise. They talk about eyeballs! We need more eyeballs—more eyeballs! A far more effective route is to carefully consider the memory you want to implant and work toward doing that. To do this, you need a story and that story needs to be compelling enough for the prospect to pay attention.

Consider the following thought experiment. Put yourself back in London in the early 1900s and you're reading the newspaper. You're flipping through while sipping your morning tea. The sound of your favorite British police sirens (eee arr, eee arr, eee arr!) can be heard in the distance. There's a cool breeze coming through the window. As you quickly flip through the classifieds only glancing at the page, something catches your eye. You spot the Shackleton ad we discussed at the start of this chapter. An ad that's only 26 words long, just slightly too long for Twitter, with no fancy graphics, just plain text, but one that stops you in your tracks. This advertisement accomplished what many of the ads in that newspaper were likely unable to achieve. It got your attention by planting a story in your head—a story of adventure, the unknown, the ability to become a hero and a legend. We can get our prospect's attention in a lot of ways, and that's why attention is an inadequate label that comes from the traditional lifecycle—because attention is in short supply. You can whack a hammer on a desk to get someone's attention. You can say something provocative and edgy, and that might do it. But there is a far more effective way, and that's to get the attention that matters.

We have a window of opportunity to plant the seed of memory and to tell a story. Stories are emotional, and they create a reaction. That's what Shackleton did with this ad, and that's what Hopkins did with Schlitz beer.

Why does this work?

Think about how you would have reacted if you had seen the ad. You would have created images in your mind about what an expedition like this would be like. It would have likely encouraged you to have images of adventure, danger, challenge, heroism, and achievement. Note that the ad threw out a few ideas like danger and honor and let you, the reader, do the rest. In other words, the ad made you make up your story by giving you a few keywords. Moreover, not only did it spell out what the job was—a dangerous expedition—it spelled out the "why" of the job—honor and accomplishment, with a little heroism thrown in for good measure.

The ad also plays on several cognitive biases. One of these is the fear of loss. The ad specified "men wanted" but it didn't mention how many. Clearly this wasn't intended for everyone, and there would surely be competition for places, despite, or perhaps because of, the difficult conditions and low pay. In fact, the ad implies that only a special sort of man could make the cut—those who didn't mind the danger, difficult conditions, and were more interested in adventure and honor rather than money. In a subtle way, it defined an in-group, and which self-respecting man wouldn't want to be part of it?

Moreover, the fact that the pay is low can be seen as an advantage. This job is about adventure and honor, and no amount of money can buy that. If it were a standard position, the low pay would be a disadvantage, but here it just highlights the special qualities and real appeal of the opportunity.

Also, this is likely to be the first time you have seen a job like this advertised and as such "anchors" all your future exposure to similar ads. So, let's suppose the next day you saw an ad for an expedition to another part of the world; you would automatically recall this original ad, which would influence your thinking and your decision about the new one.

As you can see, there are some important factors that impact the power of preemptive marketing. But what if there was another powerful tool that we could use, one that could dramatically impact the customer experience before it even happens? Well, it turns out there is, and that's the concept of anticipated memories.

A Simple Thought Experiment

Do the following thought experiment with me: I want you to think about your last vacation. I don't mean your last business trip, but a real, relaxing vacation.

Perhaps you traveled to the Caribbean, where you spent your days lounging on the white sandy beaches of Aruba. Maybe you set sail on an Alaskan cruise, where your time was spent enjoying the sights of the Alaskan snow-capped mountains, or enjoying hot coffee on the ship's balcony while watching moose and grizzly bear wandering the riverbed or the occasional bald eagle sighting. Perhaps the days passed by as you toured the vineyards of the Bordeaux region of France, sipping some of the finest wines your lips have ever tasted. I want you to close your eyes for a moment and take it all in.

Take as long as you need.

Try to remember the sights, the smells, and the feeling of the breeze on your skin. Remember the tastes of foods you tried for the first time, or the sand between your toes. Come back when you're done. Don't worry; I'll still be here.

In the few short moments it took you to complete that exercise, something fascinating happened inside your mind. It was something so profound, so powerful, and yet highly applicable to your business. What just happened, within seconds, inside that blob of jelly in your head, can drastically change how business is conducted and how organizations operate. What just happened has significant ramifications on your ability to market your business effectively, maximize customer value, and build intense customer loyalty.

Now here's something even more interesting! If you didn't close your eyes and do the exercise that I told you to do, you still, technically, completed the task.

Here's what I mean.

What happened with an almost incalculable speed is that your brain just processed through billions of tiny bits of information in an attempt to piece together a memory of your last vacation. Scientists or neurologists call this the process of recall or retrieval. Your brain used bits, pieces, and fragments of your entire vacation—whatever pieces it could pull together quickly—to create a few mental images of your last trip, snapshots if you will.

If you did complete the exercise, then you undoubtedly remembered a few very distinct and memorable things about your trip, and you could probably see certain moments replayed in your head. Your journey might have been last week—and the memories are still really fresh, or it might have been three years ago (if so, you need to take more time off!). It really doesn't matter; the same thing happened.

Now you might be wondering, "How can my recent trip to the beach exponentially change the way my organization operates?" Or perhaps you're curious how your memory can help you create a more profitable company. Then again, maybe you're just thinking, "Noah, what on earth does my last vacation have to do with customer experience, customer service, and customer loyalty?" I want to show you how with a simple understanding of anticipated memories, you can create an almost unfair advantage when it comes to maximizing your company's potential. But before we do that, we need to look at one of the most fascinating medical studies ever conducted and its implications to our discussion.

Dr. Martin Seligman, in his classic book *Authentic Happiness*, writes about an experiment involving colonoscopies:

682 patients were randomly assigned to either the usual colonoscopy or to a procedure in which one extra minute was added on at the end, but with the colonoscope not moving. A stationary colonoscope provides a less uncomfortable final minute than what went before, but it does add one extra minute of discomfort. The added minute means, of course, that this group gets more total pain than the routine group. Because their experience ends relatively well, however, their memory of the episode is much rosier and, astonishingly, they are more willing to undergo the procedure again than the routine group. In your own life, you should take particular care with endings, for their color will forever tinge your memory of the entire relationship and your willingness to re-enter it.

Before I tell you why this study is important, listen to this: Nobel Prize winner Daniel Kahneman, the author of the *New York Times* bestseller *Thinking, Fast and Slow*, who we've already talked about, coincidentally shared the same study in his own book and when he took the stage at the renowned TED Conference. I have no doubt Seligman's work influenced Kahneman and vice versa, but it's more fun to call it a coincidence.

Here we have two psychologists who were attempting to teach us about the inner workings of the human mind. One was studying the brain and happiness, and the other was studying how humans think and make decisions.

Now I already told you this, but I'm not a psychologist, and I don't play one on the Internet (or in the books I write), but here's why this matters: both of these psychologists had inadvertently stumbled upon one of the most profound business lessons ever.

Let me explain: These studies show us why customers choose to do business with one company over another. The study also shows us why they continue to do business with a business over time and why they may choose to end the relationship early, or even come back to a business after a length of time.

In a nutshell, they had discovered the secret to not only getting a new customer but how to keep them—two major issues and challenges for any business on the planet.

I've shared this fascinating medical study before. But on those occasions, I discussed how we could ensure customer and client relationships ended as positively as possible with our greatest percentage chance of being able to bring a lost customer back through customer reactivation efforts. It wasn't until I made the connection between Kahneman's and Seligman's different takes on the study that I recognized the greater implications of this research.

What this study teaches us is that contrary to the belief of marketing experts, authors, college professors, and consultants everywhere, it is not the customer's experiences that create a customer for life, or even a repeat customer, but rather it's the customer's memory of the experience. Think back to the cognitive biases we discussed earlier where we showed research that suggests that the memory is the experience. It's not *what happened* that is critical; it's *the points that we remember* that are essential. And those points will be heavily influenced by the strongest emotions we recall. So if the last part of a colonoscopy allows you to experience relief, you will have an overly positive memory of the event because it has been colored by the sense of the relief and the reduction in discomfort. And further to that, it's not your sales or marketing that gets you a customer in the first place; it's the imagination of the expected experience your customer has in relation to doing business with you. This relates back to the preemptive marketing we just discussed in the previous section.

Now you might be thinking to yourself, "wait a minute, Noah—what's the difference between the customer's experience, and the memory of the experience?" There's a huge difference. Customer loyalty becomes a function of memory, and as you'll see, even a great experience can be jaded by the reminder of the wrong memory. We don't recall a perfect memory; in fact, as one author wrote, "not only are memories capable of being retrieved, they are also capable of being reconstructed."[7]

So here's what I'm suggesting: Contrary to industry norms, the most important thing your organization is selling is not a product or service, it's not the benefit derived, and it's not even a great customer experience. But rather, it's the memories created that resonate and stick in your customer's mind—the ones that remain to be recalled and retrieved at a moment's whim—before, during, and after the sale! There's a fascinating distinction between the experience and the memory of the experience.

Here's what we've learned thus far. What we now know is that our brains work insanely hard at breakneck speeds to try to create a mental picture or a memory from billions of bits of information wedged inside the jelly-like blob inside our skulls. Unfortunately, too many organizations are leaving the creation of those mental pictures up to chance. I'm going to show you a way to ensure you're consistently creating the right memories. From the function of business, sales, marketing, support, and creating a great customer experience, this changes everything.

Kahneman says that we each experience approximately 20,000 moments each day and more than 500 million moments in a 70-year life. Obviously, we can't remember all those moments in accurate detail or even a small percentage of them. No matter how many times we're "wowed" by a company, we simply can't remember them all. Even though our brains are equipped for "big data" and packed with one of the largest storage devices ever to exist, we simply cannot capture and retain everything that we experience. That's not to say our brains aren't capable of retaining massive gigabytes of data. Our brains store gargantuan amounts of information—even memories from many years ago, including our childhood.

We can often be reminded of a memory through something as distinct as a smell, or we can often recreate the sense of smell through our own thoughts. For example, I have a distinct memory of what my grandparents' house smelled like as a child. I can remember spending many hours at their house in my childhood and the combination of my grandmother's oil paints sprawled out in the kitchen where she worked on her latest masterpiece and the mixing of that smell with the scent of her latest sweets baking in the oven. I can conjure up the memory of that smell in a moment's notice (they're coming back to me as I write this) and you can recreate a similar smell too. It's almost as if the smell is right there in front of your nose. You might have similar memories of the house you grew up in, or the chlorine from the pool where your dad took you every Saturday morning for swimming lessons, or the musty smell of Grandpa's old Ford, or the locker room at the local hockey rink. It's the same for the mental images we retain in our minds. I can remember even the smallest nooks and crannies of the house I grew up in, even though I haven't lived in that house for over 25 years.

But within those flashes of memory, there are millions of moments we simply haven't retained. And even though I can recreate a mental image of the inside of my childhood bedroom closet, where many hours were spent building forts and trying to avoid an imminent trip to the dentist, with what I feel is an exact certainty, the memories I have aren't really "exact."

My mind recreates the images to the best of its ability, piecing together as many of the stored moments as it can to create a memory; but as Elizabeth Loftus showed us, we create false memories too.

Let's suppose you're 35 years old at the time you're reading this book. If not, it's easy to do the math (take the number of days you've lived and multiply by 20,000). If you're around 35 years old, then and we can assume you've already experienced close to 250 million moments in your lifetime! If that's the case, then what has happened to most of them?

Unfortunately, most of them simply disappear. They're gone into the ether of history. Sayonara.

When we think about "experience" in our lives (a wedding day, the birth of a child, or the death of a loved one—all of which are massively emotional experiences), we still don't remember every single detail about the experience. We only remember based on whatever was stored in our minds, and those key moments that our brain deemed important to put into safe storage. We simply can't remember it all. Even then, the recall of memories is never entirely accurate. As we delve further into the book, you'll learn how to use these concepts to build an even greater competitive advantage for your organization.

For now, it's important to remember a few key things about Stage One. In this stage, we have the opportunity to introduce who we are as a company to a buyer and stoke the imagination enough that they're willing to move to the second stage.

Action Step:
Speed Is More Valuable Than Delight

1) As a prospect, visit your own website and take the action a customer would take. Perhaps they fill out a lead generation form for more information, or maybe you only have a contact form, perhaps you only have a phone number.

Whatever you have, test every form of contact as a customer and measure the response time.

If you get a voicemail, leave a voicemail and see how long it takes to get a return call.

If you get your company's interactive voice response (IVR) system, measure how long it takes to get you on the phone.

If you send a contact form, measure how long it takes to get a response.

2) Track the results and discuss them with your team. See if you can improve prospective

customer response times by 75 percent over the next 30 days.

3) Don't settle for a less than 50 percent improvement over 30 days. Improve by at least 75 percent, and then doing it again. In 60 days you should be twice as fast.

Speed is more valuable than delight.

Rid the Skeletons From Your Closet

There's a fantastic book in the world of sales that I've pillaged the following ideas from and used it to create incredible discussions with the sales and marketing teams of organizations, including some massive, billion-dollar companies. I like to give credit where credit is due: that book is called *No Lie: Truth Is the Ultimate Sales Tool,* by Barry Maher. It's a brilliant and intriguing book that I highly recommend. One of the most fascinating takeaways from that book was that it implies that some of the most powerful marketing and sales efforts in the first and second stage of the loop happen by understanding your own shortcomings and deficiencies. Maher starts the book by explaining that every product, every service, has its potential negatives. He shares the following quote from George Bernard Shaw: "If you cannot get rid of the family skeleton, you might as well make it dance." Great salespeople aren't afraid of those negatives. They don't stumble over them, and they certainly don't try to hide them. Great salespeople use potential negatives as selling points; they even brag about them.

To master the initial stages of the Customer Loyalty Loop, you need to fully understand your company's own failings and shortcomings and make the skeletons dance. Nobody's products or services are perfect. Even companies like Apple have products and services that are often plagued with problems. Maher says truth is the most powerful selling tool. The book explains that we must make our skeletons dance. When I'm working with a client on the early stages of the loop, we're looking to discover the shortcomings and areas where we can be more honest about our products and services. Remember, Stage Two is all about removing and reducing existing friction and resistance. Maher says that truth and honesty create credibility and trust. Workshopping the Skeleton Protocol can be an incredibly powerful exercise for your team. Here's how it works.

Step 1: Become your own most difficult prospect. Get your sales people together and get as honest as you can in relation to your products' and services' shortcomings. Just as FedEx did with the Hierarchy of Horrors, be brutally honest with yourself. Dig deep and spend time to understand the pain and discomfort through the eyes of your customer.

Step 2: Take all the negatives and spend time turning them into a positive. This doesn't mean listing all the positive aspects of your products and services, but ask yourself what's positive about the negative? For example, if there's a negative that you're the most expensive, then ask yourself why that is. What are all the positives for the customer in being most the expensive?

Maher gives examples like this:

Prospect: To be honest, you guys are more expensive than everyone else.

You: Of course we are! And do you know why that is? (Again, this presents a wonderful opportunity to reduce resistance and build your preemptive positioning with the prospect.)

For example, you might offer unparalleled service standards in your industry by guaranteeing someone at the client's site within 24 hours. You might have promised new parts delivered same-day across the country in the case of a breakdown.

Another example might be that you have the slowest delivery times for your products. That's likely a negative for many potential customers. But why is it a positive? Perhaps you have less breakage and fewer truck problems.

Maybe your software is old. In the eyes of a potential customer, that might be a negative. But why is it a positive? For example, maybe you can explain, "Which is exactly why our software is so stable: a well-tested, perfected, proven performer with thousands of satisfied customers and all the glitches and compatibility issues worked out."

Maher's point is that everyone else will try to use the tactical laws of persuasion to bypass that objection. But a better way, which we've discussed in great detail in the loyalty loop, is to earn the trust of that specific customer. This is a fantastic way to do it!

Maher's book provided a full-length treatment on the Skeleton Protocol, which I'm only glossing over here. If you want to read about the thinking behind it in more depth, I recommend Maher's work but here's a simple workshop that I've done with dozens of clients to address this specific issue.

Action Step: The Skeleton Protocol Workshop

Break up in teams of five to eight and work on the following exercise.

Step 1: Tell the group that they're now going to work together and role-play as your biggest competitor. Your goal is to displace yourselves.

Describe the actives, for example:

- How would we defeat us?
- How would we take our customers away?
- How would we say we're better than them?

This has as much to do with understanding the competition as it does with understanding yourselves and the potential shortcomings in your customer's experience.

Step 2: Discuss and debrief. Have everyone share how they would defeat you and the various shortcomings they notice. Have someone capture the most damaging admissions as to where you see gaps.

Step 3: Come back to reality and work as yourselves again. Work together and discuss all the negatives. Ask how you can turn each negative into a positive.

4. Stage Two: Conversion Not Coercion

Stage Two is all about the continuation of building immense trust with your prospects (which we've started in Stage One). In this stage, we take someone who has shown interest in your products or services and attempt to move them from prospect to customer. We don't do this with manipulation and cult-like persuasion techniques—far from it. If you think about traditional sales, that process is more about ringing the bell every time someone closes a new deal, and less about doing what's right for the customer to start building a long-term relationship. When you put "closing the sale" on a pedestal, you leave no room for nurturing the client, and that's a fact. It's also one of the most damaging beliefs that inhibit a company's ability to maximize customer value and build actually profitable customer relationships. And the most harmful thing of all, your customers smell it a mile away. Think of it this way: Stage One is all about showing what makes your products, your services, and your experience remarkable, exciting, and different. Stage Two is about converting the prospect into a sale, but continuing to build on the expectations of what's to come by delivering a remarkable and memorable buying—and interaction—experience each and every step of the way.

As I mentioned when introducing the loop, more often than not, customers can move through stages rapidly. The customer can move through both Stages One and Two so quickly that it seems like they didn't really happen at all. Sometimes, we have a customer who is simply ready to buy. I've had people show up on my website and just purchase. I've had people call me and spend substantial amounts of money without even really needing to talk to me. Inadvertently, these early stages of the loop have still happened; they're just not as overt as the other stages. After all, the customer heard about you somewhere. They got to your website somehow. They picked up the phone and called to place their order for some reason.

Here's a good way to think about it: Imagine a guy entering a store who needs some flowers before a hot date. In the first stage, the prospect feels like he needs to get the gift, and he sees the store as he's on his way to pick up his date. In the second stage (where we're at now), the prospect has now entered the store and is ready to buy the flowers. In this stage, the prospect must be able to find the flowers he thinks are appropriate, both quickly and easily. They must be priced accordingly, and the service representative must be knowledgeable enough to answer any questions he might have about the various kinds of flowers on sale. In essence, we're bridging the gap between the initial interest in buying from you, to the making of an actual purchase. In this case, Stages One, Two, and Three are happening incredibly fast, and that's okay.

Sales as an area of business improvement has often been treated as the "song and dance routine" between the buyer and seller. Each partner goes through a series of steps, with each reacting to each other's move, and their tactics are used to counter the effects of each other's moves. For example, "Did the prospect raise objections?" Sales training often says things like, "If so, then respond by saying one of these five things." It's tactical and focused on the wrong outcome. More important, this approach does not remove the natural resistance the customer feels in the first place, which makes it almost impossible to keep a customer coming back again and again. We'll talk about that shortly. Meanwhile, the customer is skeptical and dubious and can feel like he or she is being "pitched" or "sold."

These traditional sales approaches have gotten companies to this point, but the world has changed, and we're living in a customer-driven economy. It doesn't need to be treated like a competitive song and dance anymore, and more important, it doesn't work that well anymore, either. Moreover, as more and more is written about cognitive neuroscience and how the mind really works, consumers will become even more educated about the communication process. It might well reach a point when a sales associate says to a customer something like, "You'd better buy these because we're selling out of them fast," and the customer replies, "Please don't use the fear of loss bias on me." Or a salesperson says to a potential customer, "You may have read about our new product in the paper," and the prospect says, "I know all about the availability bias, and it's not going to work." More valuable, and increasingly necessary, is to treat the customer's movement through this stage as one of fluidity by removing friction and resistance, and setting up the customer for the latter stages. And this is an important part of the Customer Loyalty Loop as a whole. Fluidity is the key. Each stage is fluid. And the fluidity is okay, provided you understand what you might still need to do in the latter stages. Here's what I mean: If a customer picks up the phone and very quickly buys, in some cases you haven't had the chance to build trust, or to set expectations, or to do your early-stage marketing. But keep thinking fluidity. How fluid is the movement through your company's process?

When you get a lead, how quickly are they moved through the sales process and asked to buy? Do you quickly rush them through and cut to the chase and try to close the sale, or do you take a more consultative selling approach? Do you slow down the process if needed?

Cementing Trust

Stage Two is all about cementing trust and influencing the action. If you think back to the initial stage, there's already been a lot of trust building done in our early marketing efforts. We're continuing to build on that now. That's the fluidity of the loyalty loop in action. In this stage, you need to remove all aspects of friction and resistance in the sales process and move the prospect to action. This brings up an important point, and that's the common disconnect between sales and marketing. The disconnect is that there really shouldn't be one anymore, but there almost always is. Marketing departments are responsible for creating the messaging that happens in Stage One, and in Stage Two you have an entirely different group of people looking to continue the relationship and trust-building process. Another way to think about it is like this: Marketing in Stage One gets people to raise their hands, and sales, in Stage Two, gets people to open their wallets and take some action. That action doesn't have to be transactional. For example, nonprofits might work to get people to donate in Stage Two. A politician seeks a vote in Stage Two. These are all signs of action. There's obviously an incredibly important connection between sales and marketing. If that's the case, how can there ever be a disconnect between these two stages of the loyalty loop? It turns out there almost always is. One of the first things we need to do is remove those barriers and understand the fluidity and connectedness of the two stages. Creating the action in Stage Two is an incredibly important part of the customer's experience that ties directly to Stage One, and equally to the latter stages.

When I talk about the entire customer experience and the whole customer experience, this is one of the most important and often overlooked areas of focus. If you think about the first time you pick up the phone and call a business, the experience doesn't start once you pick up the phone or once you eventually get down to the store to make your purchase. The experience starts once *you* pick up the phone. Think about that for a minute. The experience starts when *you* pick up the phone, right then and there. Even then, we can argue the experience started earlier than that. At this point, the prospect has made a decision to pick up the phone and call this particular business and now your customer's experience has started. The prospect has already entered your sales process whether they realize it or not—whether you know it or not. Think about all the elements related to the customer experience that are happening the moment the customer picks up the phone for the first time. Here are a few things that come to mind:

- How many times did the phone ring before someone picked up on the other end?
- Did someone pick up at all?
- How quickly can they expect to be called back?
- Did they get a voicemail recording?
- Was the mailbox full?
- Did an automated voice system pick up asking them to select their choice? "Press 1 for support. Press 2 for sales. Press 3.... " Why don't you just tell me the movie you want to see? (Seinfeld fans will get the joke.)
- If someone answered, was the person on the other end both courteous and knowledgeable? Does that person know where to direct the customer to the next step of the sales process? You'd be shocked how many businesses direct leads to people either answering the phones or managing the e-mail that have absolutely no clue about what happens next in the process! That's just crazy.

Just a side note: You'll have to use your imagination to apply this to the various types of businesses throughout the book, because I don't have space in the book to give specific examples for every one of them; but I'll try to make it as transparent as possible as we move along. Let's continue with a few more examples:

- Is contacting you through your website a simple process?
- How quickly can they expect a response? I once e-mailed a website through their contact form, and they responded four months later. I'm not kidding. In the reply, they answered my question with another question. I'm still waiting for the next response!
- When landing on your website, is the next step clear as day, or does the customer feel like they're being dumped into a messy closet?[1]
- Is it easy for the customer to pay you? You may or may not be surprised by how many companies make it almost impossible to give them any money.

As you can see, we're already knee-deep into the customer's experience at this point. Most companies don't consider this stage as part of the customer experience because the customer isn't really a customer yet, but why? The potential customer is "experiencing" through every part of the sales process, and every interaction with your company. Your company has a goal to turn potential customers into customers, so why wouldn't you treat this with the same level of gravitas you treat the latest Snapchat campaign? It seems only logical that we would treat this as part of the entire customer experience. Just like our single, dating man buying flowers as he sets out looking for true love, the experience starts the moment he pulls into the parking lot.

Do you think about the whole customer experience?

Let's talk more about what's happening in this stage and how to ensure you're allowing the customer to move quickly to the third stage with as little friction and resistance as possible. So let's back up by starting at the beginning of Stage Two and assume our business now has a lead.

Great! Success! Stage One worked!

But uh-oh, I've got news for you.

Leads Are Worthless
. . . .

Every business wants more leads. In the traditional world of sales and marketing, leads are everything. Here's some counterintuitive thinking for you: leads are worthless. They're not worth the paper they're written on. Everyone says they need more leads, more leads, and more leads! Give me the Glengarry[2] leads! It's like we're feeding some frenzied drug addiction, but leads are worthless unless you know how to move leads from this stage to the next, and then into happily ever after, after that. More so, the very act of getting a lead is a giant waste of time and money if you haven't carefully thought through this stage of the buyer's journey and the stages that follow. As mentioned a few pages back, go ahead and drive leads to your front desk, but do you know how many leads aren't being followed up on?

Do you know how many leads receive a single call back, but no more?

Do you know what happened to the Internet leads that came in last week, or last month? How many of those leads resulted in business?

I can think of many client examples where I started looking into this and found that sometimes more than 80 percent of leads weren't even receiving a call back.

Now before you say, "Those idiots! That's ridiculous!" let me tell you that this is never that surprising to me; in fact, it's almost the norm. Most companies do a terrible job with leads and have a poor understanding of what it takes to move a lead to conversion, let alone the next stage. Leads are worthless.

Creating Gravitational Pull

Leads come in two ways: inbound and outbound. With inbound marketing, the leads come to you. They're attracted to you through your sales and marketing efforts, and they reach a point where they raise their hands and say, "I'm interested." With outbound marketing, you find leads and create opportunities through traditional sales efforts like direct mail and cold calling.

There's outbound sales and marketing efforts, and then there's gravitational pull. If you get the Customer Loyalty Loop right, the gravitational pull is far more likely to occur.

Depending on the business type, every type of lead needs to be treated differently. For example, a traditional brick-and-mortar business has a lead the moment a customer walks into the store. For a hospitality business, a lead happens when someone comes into a restaurant to review the menu before making a decision for lunch.

How many companies track their lead-to-sale ratio? I can tell you—hardly any. Here's a tip if you're in a more traditional type of brick-and-mortar business: start tracking how many people walk in the door, and how many leave with or without making a purchase. Even larger retailers need to be tracking lead-to-conversion ratio. This data will allow you to tweak, tailor, and improve this part of the customer experience.

For an online retailer, a lead might be someone who makes their way onto a website with the intent of buying and fills out a form for more information. As you see, leads come in a couple of different forms. Leads, however, are entirely worthless unless we're able to attract them in the first place, persuade them to raise their hands, and get them to trust us enough to convert to a customer. Then, we have to deliver a remarkable customer experience, and bring them back to do business with us again and turn them into an advocate for our respective businesses. Without doing all of those things, a lead is worthless. The point here is that a lead is useless unless you take them to a place of happily ever after. To bring them happily ever after, you need to understand Stage Two, which focuses primarily on your salespeople, front-line customer-facing staff, and the sales process. Everything that happens right now has the potential to impact what happens later on.

The customer is the single-most expensive thing for a business to acquire and the only real true asset a business has. For some businesses, even getting the customer to Stage Two is a huge hurdle and a massive expense. If a company wants to maximize growth, then it needs to understand the value of a lead versus a long-time relationship with a customer. Historically, companies have believed that revenue growth was simply about driving as many new customers to the business as possible and converting as many sales as they could, but it's a lousy way to do business. Every organization needs to understand the new requirements in the second stage and treat the sales process as an integral part of the customer experience.

Breaking the Loop in Stage Two

A moment ago, I mentioned the importance of the sales process. It's so foolish not to treat this as part of the customer experience. Through Stage One, you've created a mental image in the mind of the client. If we think back to the original and traditional customer lifecycle, then we've successfully created awareness. Both your advertising and marketing efforts have led the customer to this point, or maybe they've gotten here through referral or word of mouth; it doesn't matter, although not all referrals and word-of-mouth customers are necessarily good, and we'll talk about that later. Either way, think about this for a minute: Imagine the incongruence if back in the 1920s you would had read one of Hopkins' famous purity ads only to travel to the Schlitz factory and find it filthy and dirty, with bags upon bags of garbage piled outside the front door? Imagine a stream of sludge outside where you expected to find a crystal-clear basin of water flowing into the lake. There's a significant incongruity of the mental image you initially had expected between what you're experiencing. When this happens, the loop is broken. As we move into the conversion stage or the "business environment" your prospects find themselves in, we need to understand this is very much a part of the customer experience. This includes everything from the actual environment (this can be offline or online), to the people they deal with and how they're treated, and information they get from other sources.

There's one thing that can break down the entire loop. It's really scary because you can do so well right up until even after the customer has done business with you the first time, and yet you can close the casket, ensuring they'll never do business with you again. It's hard to imagine that the process can be broken any step of the way by this one thing, but it's there. And that one thing is incongruence. In other words, something that doesn't fit the overall experience, or that doesn't make sense. The piles and piles of garbage outside the Schlitz factory are incongruent, and they break down all the hard work we've done to get the prospect to that point. Let me share a brief story to illustrate my point.

Last year, I held an event for clients in Toronto. The night before the event I booked two rooms at the gorgeous Shangri-La Hotel, one for me and one for a good friend of mine and guest speaker at the event, Shawn Veltman. The check-in experience was incredible. I was whisked away from my car, which was driven off quickly by the valet parking attendants, and inside I was warmly (and magically) greeted by name. It was like they knew I would be walking in at that very moment, and everything was happening just for me. "Good evening, Mr. Fleming; it's great to have you staying with us." From there, I was given a small cup of hot Japanese oolong tea, and a hot face and hand wash cloth as the front desk attendant swiped my credit card, and finally I was escorted to my room. I turned around looking for my bags, with a slight moment of panic, only to be told my bags had already been sent up to my room. Shawn's experience was no different. He was amazed at the attention to detail throughout the entire experience thus far.

A few hours later, I met with Shawn, and he asked me a very peculiar question. He asked, "Did you notice anything distinct about the bathroom?" I pondered the question and responded, "Well, it had a TV!" Shawn said, "You're right! It had a TV, but what else?" I kept inquisitively pointing out all the distinct and interesting things I had noticed, but it seemed like I just wasn't getting it right. Finally, Shawn gave me another clue. "Noah, did you sit down to use the toilet?" I thought about it for a moment, and said, "Yeah, I did." "Great!" said Shawn. "Did you notice anything then?" I thought for a moment and then finally he blurted it out: "One-ply toilet paper." I thought about it again, and he was right. Here we were in Toronto to put on the first-ever Evergreen Summit the next day, which was all about ensuring your experiences are congruent with the story you want to tell and the things you want customers to remember about your business. The hotel had spared no expense up until this point, but then cheapened out on one small area. Let's be honest with each other here; nobody uses one-ply. It's terrible. In fact, a football team recently traveled overseas with two-ply because they were warned their hotel only carried one-ply.[3] Since I've talked about this, I've ruffled a lot of feathers. I've gotten numerous e-mails from people who claim that maybe the hotel was being eco-friendly, or people don't care about such trivial things, but they're both wrong. It's a small detail, but it's a detail that matters. The key questions to be asking yourself in this situation are these:

- Which areas of your business are you cutting costs on that might be impacting the overall customer experience and feelings your customers have?
- Where are the incongruities in your business?

I've done this work with many of my clients in the process called the Evergreen Experience Audit. We engage in many specific exercises to learn where the incongruities might be impacting the overall customer experience. We don't just look for one-ply toilet paper. We look at the whole experience and each stage of the Customer Loyalty Loop. Now the story I just shared really should be in the next chapter, after the prospect has converted to a customer and the experience has begun, but it illustrates such a valuable point for Stage Two. This is the first time major incongruities start cropping up between what you say and what you do. This is primarily true in the sales process.

Understanding Your Sales Process

When I ask many potential clients about their sales process, they sometimes look at me like I'm crazy. They say things like they don't have a defined sales process nor do they see the need for one. They say things like, "But our business is different." Here's the thing: everyone in business has a sales process. The only difference is that there are those businesses who have clearly defined each step of their sales process and those which have not. I'm not suggesting that you must have five rigid steps that are meticulously followed each and every time a new lead comes in or a person enters your business, but what I am suggesting is that your customers follow a process to the point of conversion. Moreover, you're foolish not to be aware of that process and to be continuously asking yourself the question, "How will we improve the overall customer experience at this stage?" It's all part of the whole customer experience, and this is one of the best opportunities to create added value for your customers. This value adds fuel to the fire that the customer will continue to move through the loop, resulting in sustainable long-term growth and profitability. It doesn't matter if you're a local restaurant, a freelancer, a major retail store like the Apple Store, or a complex B2B manufacturer—you still have a sales process. This chapter is called "Conversion Without Coercion" for a reason. Traditional books on sales and marketing and the psychology of influence often deal with coercion. The tools of influence are presented as tactics, and we're told that the tactics can be used throughout the sales process to coerce the prospect into buying. The Customer Loyalty Loop is focused on conversion without coercion, and we do this by making each stage of the customer experience so good that potential customers can't help but do business with us. Tools and tactics have a place in the various stages of the loop to help us move customers through each stage of the buying cycle, of course, but they're not the primary tools to move customers and prospects from one stage to the next. I look at the tools and tactics as merely a bit of added effectiveness to simply doing what you need to do to allow the customer to move freely through the whole experience. Conversion isn't really about the persuasion tactics to sell; it's more about understanding how the buyer buys and allowing them to get their own their own. In the rest of this chapter, I'll delve a bit deeper into the science of the experience in Stage Two, and we'll develop a better understanding of what the customer is feeling at this point. More important, I'll provide you with the tools to equip your salespeople and front-line staff to seamlessly move the customer through this stage to the point of conversion.

Creating an Experience-Driven Sales Process

Let's continue to think about the sales process. What are the most important parts of the experience for a potential customer in Stage Two for your business? Suppose marketing has done their job and the new lead has come in. Your salesperson's phone is ringing, or there's a new list of leads that have come in through your website. What are all the key stages, conversation points, and hurdles you must cross to get the customer to the point of conversion? How can you reduce friction, increase desire, but at the same time maintain fluidity? There was a time and place where the answer to these questions might have been pretty cut and dried, but the times have changed. Today's buyer is equipped with more research, there's more competition, and the customers have higher expectations. The sales process in most organizations hasn't been fully adapted to this new business environment. Thankfully, I can bring your organization up to speed relatively quickly. Think of this like the choreography of a Broadway show without the typical "song and dance" we just discussed. Each stage of the process should be carefully choreographed, so everyone dealing with customers hits their marks, but continues to build trust to show the customers that we have their best interests in mind. That's the difference between the conversion through manipulation and persuasion tactics, and simply allowing the customer to convert without being coerced.

If we think about our earlier discussions, including everything from cognitive biases to the formation of false memories, or stoking the imagination through the power of anticipated memories, what's left to do here? It turns out quite a bit. The experience at this stage will be remembered based on the cumulative experience of the entire sales process from start to finish. It will be recalled based on how seamless and engaging your salespeople are, or how the phones are answered (which is a soft and straightforward metric), or to how much value your salespeople bring by asking the right questions. Obviously, there are dozens of other factors. However, the more exciting thing is that if you get this stage right, it sets the foundation for long-term growth. This stage has a profound business impact on many key areas like increased revenue and customer loyalty, but only if you get it right. Achieving those results is almost impossible without a clearly defined sales process as it relates to the customer's experience. Customer loyalty isn't something that starts after the sale is made. It begins long in advance of that.

The traditional idea of selling is broken. Today's customer has so much choice that companies need to differentiate themselves from the competition. We can do that by treating the sales process as a definitive part of the customer experience. That's the problem with treating the sales process as a place where persuasion tactics can overcome what's desperately needed: value that sticks. At this stage, prospects only want to know one particular thing. They want to know that you have their best interest in mind and that you're looking to satisfy them and improve their condition. Let's talk about what that means and how we do that.

Watch Your Language

"Do you want fries with that?" The classic line that many of us heard many (too many times to admit!) before. This is part of the McDonald's script that dramatically increased the fast-food chain's business. My mentor and business coach, Dr. Alan Weiss, often says, "Language is everything. Language controls the discussion. The discussion controls the relationship. Relations controls the sale." He explains that language is one of the most important yet often overlooked aspects of running a business.

At the time of writing this section, I was at the Detroit Airport preparing to visit a client. Arriving a couple hours early, I had time to have lunch so I decided to visit a new P.F. Chang restaurant. P.F. Chang is a chain, and I've eaten at many of them before, but on this particular visit, at this particular location, I noticed something I hadn't noticed before and that was the incredible use of language and scripting. Every customer that sat down at the bar, the server said the same thing, "Hey, how's it going? I'm Janice; what's your name?" I responded and told her my name and then every time she came back, she addressed me by name. This might seem like a small thing, but I watched as nearly half a dozen customers immediately introduced themselves. Maybe it was just Janice doing this herself, but then I watched another server introduce herself in a similar fashion. It's part of their script, and it matters as part of the customer experience. It's not identical corporate language that must be followed meticulously like robots, but the intent is there. Disney Vacation Club members are greeted with the language, "Welcome home!" And when we return to the Jasmine Porch at the Sanctuary Hotel on Kiawah Island for our yearly visit, they always say, "And welcome back, Mr. Fleming." It's part of the script, part of the language, and part of the customer experience. Language and intent in the customer experience is everything. If you have three people explaining the same thing in three different ways, eventually you'll have nobody to explain it to.

Never mind the specifics, there's immense importance in talking in the language and lingo of your customer base. Starbucks created a vocabulary that their clients embraced, and Tim Horton's in Canada embraced the vocabulary their customers created for them. How well-versed are your employees to speak the language of your target market or in a language that resonates with your core customers?

I covered this in great detail in *Evergreen*, but language is incredibly important to the overall customer experience as it allows you speak to your customers in a way that resonates with them.

How about the personality of your organization? Are your front-facing people representative of the image you portray? Does the actual language used when speaking to your customers match the language used on your website, advertisements, or business communications?

One of the greatest compliments I received when writing my first book was from a well-known business book publication that said reading my book was a lot like sitting down and having a beer with me. I hope this book is the same, but you must write like you talk. And you must communicate with customers like you write.

Building Trust Through Language

In Stage Two, our goal is to cultivate trust and reduce both friction and resistance to allow the conversion process to happen without coercion. In that stage, language is everything. Just as it's important to carefully shut up and listen at this stage, it's also important to ask the right questions. Websites frequently have a section for FAQs (frequently asked questions), where the answers for the most frequently asked questions are laid out. Unfortunately, too many organizations don't properly train their people with the right language to answer those questions in personal conversations. The key focus of those initial discussions is almost always focused on what the company can do for the prospect, when it should be the complete opposite. Those initial sales encounters in Stage Two should be all about the prospect. Keep your focus on the prospect and you'll do fine. You don't have to treat this as a battle to be had amongst your potential customers.

I'm reminded of a story I heard once about a disarming sales tactic used in the jewelry and automotive sales industry. The salesperson would always start the conversion with the language, "Before we get started, do you mind if I share...." The reason to share something "before we get started" is because this presumes there's a stage before the typical persuasion song and dance, and the typical tactical persuasion efforts. The sales experts taught us that we were about to go into battle and therefore saying something "before we get started" allowed us to frame the discussion in a certain way. It's just another tactic used to circumvent resistance, instead of removing it entirely. Alas, it's still a neat little language technique that the old-school sales guys have up their sleeves.

Language is important throughout the entire customer experience, but especially important in Stage Two. Remember, prospective customers don't need to be slid down the greased chute through various persuasion tactics and techniques. Instead, we need to remove resistance and language is one of the most important tools in our arsenal to do that. What is the real purpose of an FAQ? Done right, it's to remove resistance and handle objections before they arise.

Your salespeople should be talking to customers regularly, hopefully more often than your service people, and your service people more often than your marketing people. However, I'm making an assumption that everyone is talking to customers on a regular basis. You should be starting to see how these exercises all build upon one another to create a memorable customer experience.

"Surprise, Surprise!" is a small training exercise that was developed when working with a billion-dollar manufacturing client. The goal was simple: to better understand the language prospects were using and the responses people were giving. This is not about having the perfect response to every objective, but to ensure consistency and congruency across the experience.

Here's how it worked. This team would do a weekly call where each person would share the most surprising and interesting thing they heard from a customer or prospective client over the past week. Each person would share how they responded or if they responded at all. Sometimes there wasn't that much interesting to share. Other times there were minor arguments over the right response. But more often than not, there were major "ah-ha" moments discovered and skeletons that not one sales rep had considered. There was also a glaring incongruence of typical responses to a question or concern. On more than one occasion, this has caused a problem by one person saying something to one prospect, another to a different prospect, and those prospects both eventually talking to each other.

Action Step: Surprise, Surprise!

1. Spend a few moments discussing each but of sharing, the prospect's or client's reaction to the response, and engage in a brief discussion on better ways the person might have responded.

2. Have someone collect and collate the notes.

3. If you continue to hear the same things popping up over and over again, incorporate these into the various stages of the loyalty loop. For example, a corporately shared script book could be updated and distributed regularly from sales to marketing. If there's resistance in the sales process that can be addressed in your marketing or preemptive materials, then it makes sense to work that language into the corporate language. Your customer service staff might share things that are valuable and interesting to your sales team. If things are being promised that aren't delivered in the third stage, then loyalty won't ever exist. It's impossible.

Test, Test, and Test Again!

One of the cardinal sins of all sales and marketing efforts is people don't test new ways of doing things. Some of the greatest breakthroughs with clients have come from testing. I was working once with a manufacturing client with two co-owners. I had suggested we try something and the one owner thought the idea was fabulous. The other thought it was a ridiculous waste of our time. He didn't even want to discuss it. He said they tried everything and what I was suggesting was sure to be a colossal failure. I convinced them we should test the idea. Guess what happened? We doubled (yes, doubled) the profits of the company in one year. That's pretty remarkable. The only thing I suggested was we test an idea. The cardinal rule of all sales and marketing is to continually test everything. When it comes to the four stages of the loyalty loop, there are plenty of things to be testing and constantly improving. Test your marketing efforts in Stage One. For example, run variations on your preemptive marketing. In Stage Two, test your sales efforts. For example, if you typically just respond to an RFQ as fast as possible, consider slowing down the process. If you usually send a sales rep to see the customer, test having them come to you. If you usually wait to talk to a new lead before sending them any materials, consider immediately FedEx-ing them a package of testimonials and case studies. Consider including any additional valuable information that creates your preeminent position in the customer's mind as the one and only source for their needs.

If you usually e-mail your proposals to your clients, test the process by couriering hard copies to them. Try new things always. Test everything, and test often.

Want to try and introduce a Remarkable Moment in Stage Three? Don't just spend a boatload of cash without understanding what sort of impact it has on the customer. Instead, test something new, radical, and off the wall to see what your customers are saying.

Want to implement a new follow-up process to take advantage of recency and frequency in Stage Four? Test following up at different intervals and gauge the reaction. Test the appropriate reason and appropriate time. Discover when is the single best time to ask for a review, referral, or another sale.

The point is this: Just as we can test the response to an advertisement, we should be testing our business procedures throughout the loop and constantly be looking for ways to improve the customer's experience to make it more meaningful, memorable, and valuable.

Case Study

One of my clients, Eastwood Guitars, sells to an industry that for a long time has relied on one specific model. The manufacturer makes a guitar, and the music stores sell the guitars. Eastwood, however, is also unique because it sells direct to consumer. For a long time, the small independent music stores fought against the idea of selling directly to consumers, but the tides have changed. Now some of the biggest guitar brands in the world are selling directly to their consumers.

Eastwood had spent years working to nurture and develop its customer base through remarkable customer service after the guitar had been sold from a retailer. The majority of its efforts was focused on providing useful and valuable information to its fans after the sale and continuing to build the relationship with its audience. It wanted to try something new that defied industry norms. We looked at the business model and its customer's buying behavior. Many people would buy multiple guitars from Eastwood. But sometimes a guitar would be made and it would flop. So we decided to change the model by employing a crowdfunding model within the industry. Borrowing from the likes of Kickstarter and Indiegogo, we created EastwoodCustoms.com. This way, we could gauge demand for a product before making it. The site has been a smashing success. Popular bands like Devo have partnered with Eastwood to release custom models of whacky, unique instruments. One of the first major successes for the custom shop was the La Baye 2x4 DEVO, which looks exactly like it sounds, a big 2x4 block of wood turned into a guitar. Before the Eastwood Custom Shop, CEO Mike Robinson said he might have manufactured a few dozen of the guitars and then worked hard to sell them. The Eastwood Custom presold over 250 of them before they even went into production. Not only is Eastwood selling more guitars, but they're being paid for before they're made. This is exactly the type of thing I'm talking about. Always be improving the customer experience, and *always* be looking for ways to flip the experience on its head. You never know what you'll learn.

Action Step: A/B Test Your Customer Experience

1) Make a list of all of your standard business operating procedures and brainstorm new ways of doing things. Test and try again.

2) Do the same with industry norms. Make a list of everything and anything that's considered "the way things are done in our industry." I can't tell you how many times I've heard that. Well, if you're reading this you've likely heard the term *disruption* before. It's a buzzword and I can't stand it, but if you look at every disruptive business that has gone from unknown to become a ubiquitous and dominant force in their industry, the recipe for success is almost always the same. They've taken everything that's an industry norm and flipped it on its head. Make a list of the top 10–20 things that are industry specific and brainstorm how you can do it differently.

Building Trust and Removing Resistance

There's been a lot of talk over the past few years about the changing consumer landscape. With these new changes, there have been numerous new approaches to selling introduced from consultative selling methods to challenging the prospect as a method to show your expertise. Many of these approaches are novel and on the right track, but the key to remember is that selling is no longer a method of tactics and persuasion. Instead, it's a two-way conversation and part of the whole customer experience. If you think about Stages One and Two of the loyalty loop, at this time, our sole job from a conversion point of view is to continue to build on the anticipated experience to come, continue to build on the expectations, and priming the customer to experience your products and services the right way. My mentor and business coach, Dr. Alan Weiss, often says that the consulting business is a relationship business. He's right, and in today's changing consumer landscape so many different types of businesses across various industries have had to embrace the sale as an exercise in relationship building. But when you think about it, every business is a relationship business.

When it comes to influence and persuasion, most people think of the esteemed Dr. Robert Cialdini, and for good reason. As I mentioned earlier, I've had the pleasure of having dinner and spending a couple of days with Dr. Cialdini, and he is indeed brilliant. There's no question his work has shaped the field. But there is a name that should be as recognized and as important, but is often overlooked by the same people who love Cialdini, and that's Erik Knowles. Dr. Knowles is a professor of psychology at the University of Arkansas and the one of the world's renowned experts on resistance and persuasion. Knowles, in my opinion, is best known for looking at persuasion in a new light. Knowles argues there are Alpha Persuasion strategies.[4]

These are traditional persuasion techniques that attempt to create action by doing a better job at explaining the features and benefits of something. But perhaps more compelling is what Knowles calls the Omega strategies.

Omega strategies seek to identify the resistance people have to a particular offer and remove that resistance. Omega strategies are the key to unlocking the doors to an incredible second stage of the loyalty loop.

As with Cialdini, it's important to remember that tactics cannot subsume strategy in this area. But an understanding of the work of both Cialdini and Knowles make it easy to identify jagged edges in a sales process, and make it easy to find ways to make the selling experience more natural, more comfortable, and more conducive for generating future business. To understand better, let's understand the feeling and emotions going through the customer's mind at this stage by looking closer at the work of Eric Knowles.

Removing Customer Resistance

Knowles' basic premise is simple. There are two types of persuasion. The first seeks to increase your desire for something by using the tactics of persuasion. Consider, for example, the laws of influence from Cialdini. One of those is the principle of scarcity—scarcity, meaning something is in limited supply, and you better hurry, or you might miss out. We discussed a few examples of these in the earlier discussion on the various cognitive biases companies use to get us to buy. "You'd better hurry! Only six spaces left!" "We're almost sold out." These are the Alpha strategies. The second type of persuasion, the Omega strategies, seeks to reduce resistance to purchasing by allowing the customer to move seamlessly through the process.

What is resistance? It could take different forms, but at the root, it is about the opposition to an idea or a suggestion. This is a common problem when you are trying to get people to act in a particular way, whether that is to buy your goods or even change behavior for their good. Resistance is common when you are trying to change or influence behavior.

Milton Erickson was a famous psychotherapist who practiced in the latter half of the 20th century. He was known for his techniques to overcome or, better yet, circumvent the resistance his clients had to change. As psychotherapy was developing, he was a leading proponent of the idea that you don't try to change people by giving them logical arguments and expecting them to follow your instructions just because you're the therapist. Erickson realized that if you tackle people head-on, their defenses go up, and your chance to influence them goes down. He realized that you had to work with what the client gives you and find ways to get them to own the message rather than resist it. This requires subtle communication techniques, and Erickson was the master of them. He realized that any new narrative would have a much greater chance of success if it was consistent with the person's already-existing views and stories.

There are many examples of Ericksonian wisdom in Jay Haley's book *Uncommon Therapy: The Psychiatric Techniques of Milton H. Erickson.*[5] For example, a woman in her twenties came to consult with Erickson about a major problem. The woman was frigid, and the idea of sex brought on a ton of anxiety. Erickson discovered that the client's mother had told her that sex was evil, dirty, and forbidden. Mom, unfortunately, died when the client was a preteen, and now she continued to cherish her mother's memory, which meant holding on to her edicts about sex.

The first inclination in a situation like this is to explain that the client's mother clearly had a problem and was giving very inappropriate messages about this critical part of life and personal development. However, Erickson knew that wasn't going to work because such a message was inconsistent with the client's positive views about her mother. She was very unlikely to accept such a narrative, even if any objective person could see that it was the truth. Remember, we're dealing with the mind here, and emotions are way more important than the facts. Erickson knew that he had to construct a narrative that was consistent with her mom being seen in an almost perfect light. How did he do that?

"Your mom was right," he said. "Sex is evil, dirty, and forbidden—when you're 12. Unfortunately, your mom didn't live long enough to give the 15-year-old message about sex and the 20-year-old message about sex and the 25-year-old message about sex."

Erickson then explained that he was sure that the client's wise mother would have changed the message as her daughter reached maturity. You can imagine Erickson explaining what the different messages were and concluding that her mother would surely have told her that by the time the client reached her current age, her mom would be encouraging her to have a healthy sex life. Apparently the client was able to accept this message and begin to develop a healthier attitude toward sex.

What Erickson was able to do here was to circumvent the resistance by presenting the information in such a way that the client was able not just to own the message but want to believe it. He was the master of Omega strategies.

Most companies, salespeople, and most sales training focus almost exclusively on the Alpha persuasion tactics as opposed to removing friction by embracing the Omega strategies. For example, there's a certain subset of marketers and salespeople who think of it as a greased chute. They believe, "My job is to create an experience by using all the sales persuasion techniques in my arsenal that selling is so seamless, it's like a greased chute that the customer flies down, eventually coming out at the bottom and throwing their credit card at my feet." Seamless is key, sure, but not like this. Not surprisingly, organizations that utilize these kinds of salespeople can often find difficulties in retaining those clients after the initial sale. Why is that? Well, it's quite simple. You have not reduced the friction or resistance to being sold. You've merely bypassed it, which is fine if you want one sale, but not fine if you want multiple sales and dramatically increased revenue.

Most companies will tell you that they don't do this sort of thing, they find it reprehensible, and that their professional sales staff is far above such things. They'll tell you that they focus heavily on building "value" and giving more and more value. But those same companies have sales compensation structures that all but ensure that's the behavior they're getting. My mentor, Alan Weiss, often talks about the two types of belief systems in an organization—expressed views and beliefs in action. Expressed beliefs are what you tell people you believe, what you put in your mission statements, what your PR people tell the world. Beliefs in action are how you act on a day-to-day basis. Weiss often tells a story of watching a VP scream at an employee for a minor transgression while standing within two feet of the bronze mission statement on the wall, which promised respect to all employees. This kind of disconnect is depressingly common and can be seen in many departments, but rarely is it so destructive as in a sales department.

This is because though organizations often talk about wanting full collaboration between departments, and talk about wanting to create long-term customer satisfaction and value, the reality is that the sales department is often rewarded based on their hunting ability—the ability to close a new deal, meet aggressive quotas, get more new clients. We've all seen the stereotypical image of a salesperson "ringing the bell" after getting a new deal in pop culture, and many of us have seen it in our offices, but how often have you seen the alarm that goes off when a customer leaves? Not very often, I'd guess. In fact, most businesses aren't even listening for that alarm. Their ears have been trained only to hear the ding of the bell. More important, how often have you seen bonuses rescinded when a new customer never comes back? If the compensation structure is geared toward new customer acquisition, then you've told your team in no uncertain terms that customer acquisition is the most important thing happening in your business. Sad, but true. Let's continue to focus on reducing friction and resistance by treating this part of the buying experience in the context of the whole customer experience.

When someone moves from Stage One to Stage Two, they're still not entirely convinced. They are intrigued, sure, but they're not totally sold or ready to move forward. Stage Two, as mentioned, is about continuing to build trust and remove resistance. Knowles' work in influence and persuasion is perhaps far stronger than that of Cialdini's these days because you remove resistance not just during the sale, but after the sale as well. Consider again, the customer who has slid down the greased chute with all the powerful persuasion techniques of the stereotypical salesperson. What's the first thing a customer feels after purchase? Almost always, they feel buyer's remorse. In much of my work with clients, we have to work reactively because they have retention problems, and the retention problems stem from the expectations gap to the greased chute, to the use of the wrong persuasion techniques. When reducing resistance and friction early, we remove almost all of the buyer's remorse that crops up. When you drive a customer without conscious thought about what happens on Stage Two, then you've missed a lot of important steps that cause more problems later. The customer is convinced that they're making the right choice and companies are no longer left dealing with the proverbial questions of "Why are our customers leaving us, and what can we do about it?"

Customers don't spend all their time thinking about opening up their wallets for our companies. The problem with only using the tactical persuasion techniques is that though we might move a customer to the third stage and create the action or the intended conversion, we don't remove all reluctance, indecision, and upcoming remorse. It's almost impossible to create customers for life, or even happy, delightful, raving fans if you're not carefully considering that in this stage.

Three Types of Resistance
· ·

Knowles argues that there are three types of resistance. The first, he says, is reactance. Reactance is the resistance against the persuasion process itself. People aren't idiots. They know when they're being sold and pitched, and they resist it. They react by essentially saying, "Look, I understand what you're trying to do here, and I don't like it! Leave me alone."

If you think about today's digitally connected world, is it any surprise that this might be the single largest driver of customer resistance? Think of the last time you stepped foot on a new car lot. You see the salesman from outside; he narrows in on you like an eagle stalking its prey, and he starts walking toward you. Furniture stores are incredibly guilty of this. You walk in, and you're swarmed by a hungry seller hoping for a small bump in commissions on her next paycheck.

We've all felt this type resistance to the sales experience, and we react to it. It's only more amplified today, and you need to be aware of it if you are interested in increasing customer loyalty. Contrast that to Elon Musk and Tesla, who have removed almost all friction from the buying process, by effectively letting you build your car online and press the checkout button without ever having to talk to a salesperson. This is what I'm talking about when we talk about the science of the customer experience. How much reactance–resistance are your selling efforts creating? Is your sales process built on the tactics of persuasion to move the customer to action, or do you work to remove the resistance early?

The second type of resistance is skepticism. We've all felt skepticism about an offer. You've heard the line "If it seems too good to be true, it probably is." Clever marketers have used influence techniques to blast past the skepticism resistance, but you'll never create a long-term loyal customer if that's the case. They feel it. Deep within their souls, the feeling of skepticism will always linger. Skepticism isn't always deceptive. Sometimes it's simply the feeling that "You know, this product looks great, but I'm not sure it's the right one for me." Again, in Stage Two we have an excellent opportunity to deal with skepticism by understanding it's there and building our customer experience and sales process to ensure it's always dealt with before the sale, rather than after.

The third type of resistance is inertia. Knowles argues that this type of resistance isn't caused by the persuader but by the prospect herself. Knowles says this is as disappointing for salespeople as it feels like their prospects are being rude, unresponsive, and so on. In those cases, it's more likely that the other causes of resistance are the reason why they're holding out. Salespeople that call too often and follow-up too much, for example, start to seem desperate. I've made this mistake numerous times in my career. I haven't dealt with the reactance or skepticism, and I've lost the business because of it. Or, I've moved a customer through without dealing with it only to have to deal with it later. But in the case of inertia, it's often the one being persuaded who is reluctant to change. It's important to gauge for this early on. Don't get me wrong. Time is money, and if someone has no plans on taking action or creating a chance, we can't stick around forever. But even then, there's an excellent opportunity to create an experience that's engaging and memorable enough that when the prospect is ready, we'll be top of mind. Remember, it's all a relationship business now.

So here's an important question: If our customers feel all this resistance as they move from Stage One to Stage Two, what's the most efficient thing we can do to move to conversion without coercion? We've already established the importance of building trust, but another method of dealing with resistance is to acknowledge it in the first place. So many sales and marketing experts have been using these boardroom buzzwords of "authenticity" and "transparency" over the past couple of years, without actually telling us what they mean when they say that. Around the back door, I think what they're trying to say is that people have become increasingly immune to tactical persuasion, and this is one way to overcome resistance—by simply speaking the truth.

Removing resistance is the key to Stage Two. Instead of asking ourselves how we can better persuade and convert tactically, we need to be asking how we can better provide value to the customer at this stage. What if you redefine the conversion process by stressing the importance of a long-term relationship with your customers early on?

For example, as a slight digression, here's a "tactic" you can start using right in Stage Two. Consider this question often asked at many businesses at the time of conversion: "And how did you hear about us?" The reason they're asking this question is pretty simplistic. They want to collect marketing data. It's pretty straightforward Marketing 101. If 10 people told you they heard about you from a friend, and 90 people said they found out about you on Facebook, that's pretty significant in terms of where to invest additional marketing dollars. But here's the tactic you can use that continues to build on the fact that you not only think in terms of a long-term relationship but also that people refer you. Instead of asking, "And how did you hear about us?" change the language to "And do you mind if we ask who referred you to us?" If they give you someone's name, you say, "That's great! Thank you so much for letting us now. We'll be sure to thank her." But if they say, "Nobody. I saw your ad on Facebook," here's your opportunity for a slight reframe. You respond by saying, "Oh, that's odd, because 90 percent of our business comes from word of mouth." What you're doing here is planting the seed for future referrals (that they're somewhat expected and common). More important, you're also implying that your customers must be so happy with your products and services that a long-term relationship with your firm is the norm and that you expect them to be so thrilled that they'll be routinely telling others about you.

The Psychology of Guarantees

We'll talk later about guarantees and the "risk-free for 30 days" types of offers that we're all familiar with, but it's important to take note of why these work specifically well in Stage Two to remove resistance and friction from the conversion process itself, and how you can make them even more appealing in your business. There have been lots of different types of guarantees used in business over the years. Everything from the money-back guarantee to the risk-free guarantee, to the satisfaction guarantee, to the lowest price possible guarantee and many more. In the past few years, we've seen more extreme examples of guarantees used with great success. For example, Zappos became best known for its massive 365-day return policy. Identity theft protection company LifeLock offered a $1 million guarantee to its customers in the event of identity theft. This guarantee in particular, however, was squashed when the FTC (Federal Trade Commission) decided it was deceptive in nature. LifeLock was sued by the FTC for $100 million, and the FTC won. Don't let this scare you away, though. When used properly, guarantees are an especially powerful tool in the second stage of the loyalty loop, and I'll show you how to do them right.

There's only a few simple questions we need to answer about guarantees to build them for almost any business. And before you say, "We could never use guarantees in our business," think again. I could make a case and provide examples of guarantees and risk reversal to be used in any type of business. To create an effective guarantee, you first need to find all the reasons your customers might not be buying, and then create guarantees to alleviate those concerns. The goal of risk reversal and guarantees is to give your prospects 100 percent certainty and assurance in their decision-making process.

Why Do They Work?

It's really quite simple. You take nearly all the risk off the customer's shoulders. Every time a prospect is faced with a buying decision, the mind almost instantly starts resisting.

In my consulting practice, I charge high fees for an incredible ROI. I also offer a strong guarantee. If we have not met the mutually agreed-upon objectives, I'll consider working until we do. If we are still unable to meet the mutually agreed-upon objectives, I will refund your entire fee in full. By the way, if you're reading this now and want to see how I can help your business, that's a pretty remarkable guarantee! You'd be foolish not to put the book down and call or e-mail me right now...just saying.

But the guarantee removes all the risk from my potential client's shoulders and puts it all on mine. Marshall Goldsmith is the most well-known CEO coach in the world. A coaching assignment costs over $250,000, but Marshall allows you to pay at the end of the assignment, only *if* positive change has occurred. The catch? The client being coached doesn't decide if positive change has occurred, their key stakeholders do. This might include a wife, a spouse, coworkers, or others. Marshall is confident in his approach. I'm confident in my approach. How confident are you in your approach?

Guarantees work because they indicate that you're incredibly confident in your products, your services, their performance and quality, and your ability to service and delight the customer. It's not much more complicated than that. But if you also remove the investment risk, it makes things a heck of a lot easier for your prospective clients.

For example, the Lands' End guarantee reads as follows:

GUARANTEED. PERIOD.*

The Lands' End guarantee has always been an unconditional one. It reads: "If you're not satisfied with any item, simply return it to us at any time for an exchange or refund of its purchase price."

We mean every word of it. Whatever. Whenever. Always. But to make sure this is perfectly clear, we've decided to simplify it further: Guaranteed. Period.*

It's more than a return policy. It's a promise we've kept for over 50 years now, to stand behind every product we make and every service we deliver.

Now that's what I'm talking about! The key objective here is simple. By taking away the risk of the transaction, you reduce resistance and make it easier for the prospective customer to say "yes." That doesn't mean you use risk reversal or guarantees in place of a remarkable customer experience. Creating value isn't just about giving more; you create value by reducing resistance and buyer's remorse for your client. I guarantee it.

Action Step: Satisfaction Guaranteed

What type of guarantees are you offering? How could you remove the risk for your customers? What is the leading cause of resistance for your customers? What objections do you hear most often from your customers?

Step 1: Ask yourself, what are all the risks involved for the customer when buying from us? Sometimes it's easier to ask your customers what they're feeling. For example, are they concerned they won't like the product? If they having pricing concerns, ask yourself why this is—is there a competitor who offers a similar product at a better price? If this is the case, you might need to be asking what you can do to differentiate yourself from the competition. What are your customers afraid of? Are they concerned the product might break? Are they concerned they might not like the product or change their mind? This will help you better determine the type of guarantees your company should offer. List every objection, fear, and concern the potential prospect might have. Be prepared to answer them, and then back them up with your guarantees.

Step 2: In conjunction with a guarantee, ask yourself the following questions. How can we reduce the customer's fears and objections? Remember, the more you can do before the sale, the less you have to worry about after the sale. The reason many companies need guarantees is they aren't doing enough of the grunt work in the earlier stages. I much rather prefer guarantees that not only reduce risk but back up the positioning of market dominance and product superiority: "We are so convinced this will be the best mattress you've ever slept on, go ahead and sleep on it for 100 days. If at that point you're not convinced, no problem. Just call us up and you'll get a full no-questions-asked refund." Now that's what I'm talking about.

Step 3: Create your guarantees. I believe that if you're selling something that you can't fully guarantee, then you shouldn't be selling it in the first place. Imagine if everyone backed up what they promised in sales and marketing, and then lived by their guarantees! What a world we could live in. Create powerful guarantees with strong emotional language. For example, it's easy to say, "All of our guitars come with a 30-day return policy." But that's rather boring. It's a lot more interesting to say something like, "Go ahead. Plug the guitar into your own amp, use your own pedals. Take it on the road with you. Jam with it. We know that buying a guitar online isn't easy. It might look nice, but that's a lot different than using it on your terms. Go ahead and try it for the next 100 days. If you're not absolutely convinced at the end of those 100 days that you've made an incredible investment, go ahead and send it back to us. We'll pay the shipping and either send you another guitar, or refund your money in full." Which guarantee is more valuable to you? Make your guarantees bold and emotional. Guarantees aren't about stating policies and a lame mission statement on the wall about customer satisfaction; they're a moment to tap deep into the emotional state of your prospective customer.

Step 4: Now improve your guarantees by reducing even more risk. Make it virtually effortless for the customer to take advantage of the guarantee. Too many companies offer guarantees and then fill them with fine print that essentially voids the impact the guarantee had in the first place. Make it fuss-free. Learn why the customer is unhappy or asking to take advantage of the guarantee, and give the guarantee. Now, a moment ago I mentioned that in my own guarantee, I offer to refund in full the entirety of consulting projects. I also mention that we will meet mutually agreed-upon objectives. My entire business relies on my relationship with the buyer. We have a crystal-clear discussion about the desired outcomes and create agreed-upon objectives. It's not a loop hole, it's more about doing my due diligence in advance. But at the end of the day, if the client isn't pleased, I will refund their money. In my 12 years of business, I've never once been asked to give a refund. If you offer a money-back guarantee, send the money the day the request is received. Don't create tons of hoops for the customer to jump through. If the customer is unhappy, you're only creating more animosity after the fact.

Step 5: Want a winning guarantee? Here's the single-most powerful way to do it: Look at every major competitor in your industry and create the single-most powerful guarantee in the industry. That's how you win. That's how you make it a no-brainer. That's how Zappos dominated the shoe industry. That's how Walmart dominated the lowest-price retail industry. That's how Dominos dominated the pizza industry. And that's how Lands' End dominates with my favorite guarantee around.

Changing the Dynamic of the Relationship
. . . .

You remove resistance from the sales process by shifting from sales persuasion to collaboration. There's been a lot of talk of the consultative or challenging sales approach over the past few years, and rightfully so. Instead of presenting the sale as a jousting match, you approach it as a partnership. Your front-facing people need to become trusted advisors, consultants, and guides. Your goal is to guide the client to their desired outcome—one that improves the client's condition. Here's a better way to think about today's customer and today's marketplace. Customers have a better radar for techniques. They smell it, and it turns them off. But if you approach every relationship with one of real intent that you strive for long-term relationships, and you have their best interest in mind, they've got a radar for that too. Many salespeople have gotten a bad rap, but rightfully so.

I'm going to assume you've successfully removed all resistance (and don't worry, in the third section of the book I'll give you specific tools to build your sales process experience and actual language you can use), and the prospect has now officially converted to a customer. Now we're going to move on to the third stage of the loyalty loop where we're delivering your product or service.

In the overlap between sales and marketing, the balance needs to be struck between presenting your products in the most appealing way but also building a relationship with your customer. The binary brain once again rears its two-sided head and can make us believe that presenting your products and building a relationship are somehow two different activities. Ideally, they are not.

When you are doing the former, you are doing that in the context of an ongoing interaction with the customer. And when you're relationship building, the customer is typically mindful that this is a sales interaction. I'm reminded here of crowdfunding campaigns.

Anyone with knowledge of crowdfunding platforms knows that typically you can't just put up a video of your product and expect people to donate to the cause, whatever it may be. What you're trying to do, first and foremost, in a crowdfunding campaign is to gain fans. A crowdfunding platform is a place where you can showcase your stuff in a way that develops a fan base. Once someone is a fan, they are much more likely to reach into their pocket. So, in almost every business transaction, there's a delicate balance between presenting your goods and developing a relationship—and that is what the Customer Loyalty Loop is all about.

The Psychology of Testimonials

Remember the lines repeated many times in this book. Logic makes people think, but their emotions make them buy. They buy on emotion but justify those decisions with logic. In Stages One and Two, we're tapping deep into the customer's emotions. Testimonials are one of the most powerful tools used to demonstrate your ability to provide value to your clients. It's one thing for you to say it in your sales and marketing efforts, but it's another for your customers to say it for you. In this brief section, we'll look at how to obtain and create compelling testimonials, what a testimonial should include, and where to use it. The more trust you present in the earlier stages of the loop, the better job you'll do at obliterating any resistance as the prospect moves to the third stage. As mentioned in Stage Four, the very act of gaining testimonials is part of that stage, but now I'll show you how to get them. More important, I'll show you to put a system into place to gather testimonials in a systematic manner and where to use them in your sales and marketing efforts. I can draw a direct correlation between specific testimonials and a lot of revenue in my own business. Let's briefly discuss why testimonials work.

Why Do Testimonials Work?

When I wrote my first book, I realized I was entering a new phase of my business. For starters, my business had done well, but outside the client base and work I'd done in the previous years to attract business to me, I was now putting myself out there for people who had never heard of me. When you write a book, your publisher asks you to get endorsements. Endorsements are a lot like testimonials. After all, if this person is willing to vouch for this other person, or say their book is worth reading, then it must be worth reading. I decided to go right to the top of the business world and seek endorsements from one of the most influential people in business, and that was Seth Godin. Seth and I had met a few times at previous events, but beyond basic pleasantries that was about it. I attached my manuscript to an e-mail and hit "send," sending to Seth. In less than an hour, I got a response from Seth. He explained that, as I could probably imagine, he gets a ton of books and would try to take a brief look in the coming weeks. Less than 24 hours later, I was driving when I saw a notification on my cell phone. It was a response from Seth. I pulled over and read the response. Not only had he read my book, but he had even disagreed with a few of my points and wrote very articulate reasons for why he disagreed. Then, he explained what he did agree with and at the end of the e-mail was an endorsement.

Gaining testimonials are incredibly important. They're even more important when they come from influential companies. These are one of the highest-impact, lowest-cost business growth tools available to almost any business. I remember once speaking to another consultant who told me fascinating stories about the time she consulted with Apple. She told fantastic stories about working with the company and spending time in the boardroom. I asked her if she had a testimonial from them, and she did. I then looked at her website and found no Apple logo, no mention of her work with Apple, and no testimonial. Do you think this small tidbit of information might do a lot to alleviate resistance from prospects in the early stages of the loop? Of course it world. I asked her why she would do this and she said it felt a bit like gloating. She was also afraid people might not believe her. This is such nonsense. When I e-mailed Seth Godin, I figured the worst thing that could happen would be that he would say no. He said yes. Who are the exemplars in your business or industry that could provide you with a fabulous testimonial or endorsement?

Action Step: Solicit Great Testimonials

The goal of a great testimonial is to reduce friction and solidify a prospect's decision in the second stage of the loop. Here are the only things you need to know about a great testimonial:

- The testimonial should show the before and after of doing business with your company.
- It should tell a story.
- It should use specific and concrete examples. You don't want your customer to say, "The experience was great and we saved a lot of money." You would rather have them say, "Our experience working with Noah was so good. In fact, his recommendations saved us $127,450 in the first six months of working with him!" That's a real comment, by the way, from one of my clients.

How Many Testimonials Do You Need?

You should be soliciting them regularly so they're new and fresh. If it's 2016 and I'm looking to have you rebuild my web presence, the last thing I want to see is testimonials from 2004 when AOL was bombarding everyone's mailbox with CDs. I'm all for quality over quantity, but it should be part of your post-customer follow-up to request a testimonial, a review, or specific feedback for your work and the experience they've had with you.

Where to Use Them?

You should be using them everywhere. There's no bad place to use them as they have impact during each stage of the loyalty loop. In Stage One, they cause the prospect to pay more attention. In Stage Two, they make your sales process more believable. In Stage Three, they help solidify the prospect's decision, making them more likely to enjoy the experience. And in Stage Four, the client is more likely to give one if they've seen many others. Use them on your websites. Use them in your outgoing customer communications like quotes and proposals. Use them on your brochures and in your advertising. Use them in your regular, nonpromotional material to clients. You get the idea. Don't send anything out without a testimonial on it. The psychology of testimonials is really quite simple. Prospects are skeptical, cynical, and resistant to sales efforts. Testimonials work to break down those walls. I looked, but I can't find a great business that isn't using them (Apple, Zappos, Amazon, GE, etc.) but I easily found over 50 small business websites that were not.

I once heard a marketer say that 10 great testimonials will trump 100 years of positive business history. I believe it.

Acquire them, and use them.

5. Stage Three: Experience Choreography

Who is the most important person in the hotel?

If you guessed the doorman, you got it right. The doorman is the single-most important point of contact in the hotel, and the reason for that is this: She is almost always the first person the customer sees and the last person the customer sees. These days, one of the things I like to say is that everyone in the organization is the doorman. Everyone can impact the first and last impression.

If you think about how this relates to any business, it's quite simple. First impressions are more important than ever before. But at this stage, we're assuming the prospect has officially moved from prospect to customer. The customer has already had many moments and opportunities to engage with your company, but at this point, their stature has changed. There were other first impressions and moments of the experience that mattered. But at this stage, the customer has been influenced to complete the sale and now has an expectation that you'll deliver on the promises made in the previous stages. More on that shortly, but first let's talk about how customer service plays a role in each stage of the loop but becomes even more important in Stage Three.

Every company says they put the customer first. Every one of your competitors says they deliver "remarkable customer service." Everyone. Find me a business that doesn't say they provide extraordinary customer service. It's a sham, and it's a sham because it's rarely true. What companies say versus what they do is rarely congruent. If it were true, we'd have no need for sites like Yelp, TripAdvisor, or Google Reviews. The majority of review sites exist solely for someone to air their grievances for when what they were promised, or what was expected, wasn't what was delivered. Are the reviews always valid? Of course not. There are valid complaints and there are invalid complaints. And there's there are sites like Yelp and others that have developed and morphed into mini-communities of foodies and groups of people with shared interests who like to share the experiences— good, bad, or other. It just seems that the bad almost always outweighs the good, and rightfully so. But some of the horrific reviews and almost unbelievable customer service stories we hear about are incredibly valid.

Almost 80 percent of the work I do with my clients revolves around the concept of the expectations gap, which is the gap between what a customer is sold and what they actually receive. When you fix that, you dramatically increase profits and customer lifetime value. Sometimes the gap is created through overzealous sales and marketing efforts, and other times it's because the actions of the company simply can't live up to the vision and expectations of upper management. When I speak to audiences, I often share the story of a hypothetical bank to illustrate the expectations gap. Here's an easy way to understand it:

> The CEO believes the bank exists to provide solutions for their clients and to be a financial services partner. The rest of the executive team buys this, and the CMO ensures the marketing messaging matches this belief.
>
> The customer, however, believes the bank is just the place to store his funds while he waits for the mortgage and electricity bills to be paid on time.
>
> Finally, the teller believes her job is just to smile and ensure she does the best she can to keep the customer satisfied.

As you see, we have three very different sets of expectations creating one major problem—a huge gap. Almost every organization I start working with has a massive expectations gap. Here's another way to think about it: Every organization says that they provide solutions to other's problems. Everybody says that they're near perfect. But companies, like people, often exhibit a huge gap between what they say and what they do. There's often a breakdown between the things the company says in its mission statement on the walls and its About Us page on a website.

Consider the following study from the 1970s where two prominent social psychologists (Darley and Batson) set out to try and better understand what influences people to help others. They carried out their study by testing the classic Bible parable of the Good Samaritan.[1] In the

Bible story, a man is found lying on the streets beaten and bloodied by a bunch of thugs. A priest and another man both approach the man but just step over, not offering any help. Imagine that! Finally, another man who would have been considered an enemy to the hurt man stops to help and offers care. He is labeled the Good Samaritan, and this is where the line about "love your enemies" comes from. We expect the priest to stop. After all, here is a man who has supposedly devoted his life to helping others, but the priest couldn't be bothered even though it's evident the man was in dire need of assistance.

The two social psychologists considered the parable for a long time and then asked a smart, but very simple question. Is it possible the priest and the other man were just busy? Is it possible they were in a rush and had somewhere to get to? Maybe the priest was late for a wedding ceremony! It seemed like a valid question, so they decided to recreate the study using a group of seminary students.

The groups of seminary students were invited to take part in a study that was happening at a particular place at a certain time. When they arrived at the study, the researchers told them that the study had been moved to another room across campus. One group of students were told they had to get there quickly because the study was starting so they better hurry. Another group was told the study would begin when they got there, so there was no need to rush over.

Along the way, the seminary students would encounter an actor, directly in their path on the ground with his eyes closed, violently coughing and clearly in need of assistance. What do you think happened? Would the students stop to help? Would they ask the man if he was okay?

Not exactly. In the study, only some seminary students stopped to help. But less than two-thirds did, and only 10 percent of those who were told they were in a hurry stopped to help.

It seems that no matter how they would describe themselves to their friends and family on their weekends away from school, as soon as a minor inconvenience cropped up, they threw out their espoused values of helping others and busily hurried on their way.

It seems that it's rather easy to find excuses not to live our true values, whether personal or corporate. Many company mission statements say things like, "We put quality and customer service above all else," but frontline experiences often seem directly antithetical to our lofty vision statements. And this study points out the reasons why: it's easy to ignore our higher motivations when there are pressing personal concerns or there's a gap in the expectations throughout the organization. It's easy for companies to say that they're committed to creating world-class customer experiences and to ensuring that everyone throughout the organization continues to improve their skills in these areas. But when budgets are tight, and deadlines loom, it's also easy to put these goals aside and ignore learning opportunities for just getting through the current busyness, or dealing with the latest business emergency (as if another one won't pop up next week!).

Every company says it's a learning organization, and every company says that it puts customers first, but that's usually not true. In this chapter, we'll dive into the experience after the prospect has become a customer and what you need to do to ensure your team isn't just stepping over customers. Just as incongruities can kill a business when Stage Two differs from Stage One, they can show up here again, and cause equal and perhaps far more damage. In the rest of this chapter, we'll talk about what's expected here and how to ensure you're meeting those expectations. Here's the best part: it's often quite simple to excel in this stage because so many organizations are so bad.

Experience Your Competitors

When Tom Monaghan, the founder of Domino's Pizza would travel, he would always look in the hotel's phone book and order pizza from a few of the local pizza businesses. When Sam Walton traveled, he would visit Kmart stores to see what he could steal for Walmart. Walton took a notepad and would make meticulous notes as he carefully walked through the stores. He would talk to customers, and he would talk to the employees. He would then take what he learned back to Walmart and see where they could instantly improve. Too many of us look at the competition as a threat instead of looking at the competition as a way to learn. Monaghan was interested in learning how the pizza was boxed, what the delivery cars looked like, how the ordering process was handled, what the pizza looked like when it arrived, and so on.

Others look at the competition and think they understand what they're doing. They assume that because they're selling a similar product or service, they must be using similar sales efforts, and delivering a similar customer experience. In my experience, this is one of the most valuable ways to improve your business. Talk to your competitors. Shop their businesses. Talk with your suppliers about your competitors. Learn as much as you can. More important, experience it for yourself.

For example, I've been conducting a little test lately. I call various companies and leave a voicemail. I send in contact forms on websites and wait to get a response. These are all businesses I've never done anything with. Then, I repeat the process with companies where I've actually made a purchase and I'm a client. If I see they're active on social media, I'll hit them up there and tell them that I've filled out a contact form or left a voicemail, and I'm waiting for a response. And then what happens is I usually wait, and wait some more after that. What I've found is that the speed of follow-up from many companies is, for the most part, downright horrendous. I strongly believe that just being fast is more valuable than trying to be delightful and cute. I'm not talking about complaints, which we'll talk about in another section; I'm talking about general inquiries made in every stage of the loop. Remember, the customer experience has less to do with being delightful, and surprising at times, but more to do with being good across the board. In fact, the less effort and more speed involved in getting help, providing an answer, or responding to an inquiry, the more business you will do. It's that simple. This action is relatively simple, yet extremely powerful. It ties into the Evergreen Experience Audit but warrants its own action step. Measure your speed of response. If you don't want to do this yourself, hire someone from outside your company to do it.

Visit your competitors' websites and fill out their contact forms. Just like Sam Walton and Tom Monaghan would do, buy from them. See what the experience is like across the entire Customer Loyalty Loop. How do they follow up post-sale?

A client of mine wanted to complete this exercise by using their largest competitor as the case study. We essentially completed an Evergreen Experience Audit on their biggest competitor. When we were done, we reported our finding to the client's sales team, but we didn't tell them who we were talking about. We asked them to review and evaluate the experience and let us know what we thought.

Nearly everyone thought the experience sounded remarkable and almost all of them were convinced it was a narrative of doing business with them. When we explained it wasn't about them, but instead it was their largest competitor, and then we compared their customer experience with them, there were a lot of unhappy faces in the room. They were only doing about a quarter of what the competitor was doing to please the client.

Remember, my goal as a consultant to my client is to improve their condition, even it means a few people will be discomfited by the findings. In this case, the entire sales team wasn't loving me at this very moment.

But this wasn't about saying the competitor was doing more; it was about seeing what my client could do even better. Both Walton and Monaghan knew there was always something they could be doing a little bit better. They just knew that it sometimes meant looking under a roof that belonged to someone else.

Action Step: Competitive Intelligence

Step 1: In the next five minutes, see if you can learn something about your competition that you didn't know before. Ask yourself if what you've learned is a practice you can borrow, improve, or adapt to your company, division, or current efforts.

Step 2: Create a plan to do an in-depth study on your key competition. You may need to utilize outside sources. You can engage friends and family or outside experts. Use your findings to compare the competitor's experience to your experience. Create the narrative of the whole customer experience and see how your experience matches up. Look at it across the various key areas of the customer experience, before, during, and after the sale. Know the customer inside and out. Below are some things to look for.

- Who are your main competitors?
- What unique strategies are they pursuing that you're not?
- What unique sales and marketing methods are they using that you're not?
- How does their website compare to yours?
- Is it a messy closet or neat and organized?
- Do they have a mailing list?
- What happens after you join their mailing list?

- Do they offer testimonials, guarantees, or case studies on their website?
- Do they have a unique selling proposition on their website?
- How do they position themselves in Stage One of the loyalty loop?
- Do they have a customer service phone number?
- Does someone answer?
- How long does it take before someone answers?
- Do they have a storefront or office space?
- What's like it?
- Describe the curb appeal.
- If it's a retail space, how is the store laid out? Is it brightly lit, are you greeted quickly, or do they have music playing? Take note of the sights and smells.
- What is their selling process? How does it differ from yours?
- Can you talk to their customers?
- Can you ask them about the experience before, during, and after the sale?
- Do they post online reviews? If so, what do they say?
- How do their core products and services differ from yours?

You get the idea; those are more than a dozen questions I rattled off the top of my head. If it were me, I'd be looking at everything my competitors are doing, particularly the experience as a customer and how they follow up after the sale. Don't view the competition as a threat; instead, view them as an opportunity to learn. After all, they're your competition, which means they're making money from people who should be buying from you.

Shocking Dogs

One of the all-time bestselling books in the business world is the catchy *Good to Great* by Jim Collins. How hard is it to go from good to great? What if you could go from okay to exceptional without really having to change much at all, except having a better understanding of the Customer Loyalty Loop and your ability to meet the customer's expectations across each stage of the loop? Geez, for many businesses just going from dismal to good could perhaps be the difference in creating a dump truck full of additional revenue. Look, I'm not saying you're dismal. But the progression is Dismal to Good > Good to Great > Great to World-Class.

One of my clients runs a successful dog day care business in Detroit. When I suggested during a coaching call that we start shocking her clients' dogs in the name of science and the customer experience, the phone went silent. I was joking, of course, but one of our favorite social psychologists, Dr. Martin Seligman, wasn't when he engaged in such a study in 1965.[2] His findings have profound ramifications for the entire Customer Loyalty

Loop and show us that getting customer service right across the entire loop doesn't need to be difficult, but it's remarkably important. In fact, it offers us the greatest opportunity to go from good to exceptional incredibly quickly.

Seligman's experiments involved putting dogs into a small enclosed room where the animal would receive electrical shocks that they couldn't do anything about. The researchers would ring a bell and then shock the dog. The idea was simple; the dog would become conditioned to associate the sound of the bell with the unpleasant shock. At first, the dog would attempt different behaviors to try to find a solution. It might try to get out, or hop over a small fence to avoid the shocks. But that's not what happened. As each shock occurred, the dog became more helpless. Eventually, the dog would just give up and not try anymore. Even when the conditions were changed, and the dog could avoid the shocks by completing a simple action (like hopping over a fence), the dog would do nothing. They would lie down and take the shocks. Why? Because the dog had learned (and been convinced) that nothing would help, so there was no point in trying to escape its fate, meaning that even when escape was available, the dog would not try to avoid the shock. This became the concept known as "learned helplessness." Learned helplessness can be defined as the situation in which the individual learns that they can't escape some negative situations. So even if the circumstances change, they can't be bothered to change.

The work on learned helplessness was extended to other contexts. For example, in one study subjects did a mental task in the presence of distracting noise. One group of subjects could switch the noise off and another group could not. Interestingly, the former group rarely turned off the noise, but their performance was far better than those in the helplessness group who had no such control and did the mental task in the presence of the noise, too. The explanation is that the former group had control over the noise, and it was this sense of control that differentiated the group's performance. As we know, lack of control is the toxic element of stress.

The Helpless Customer

This concept of learned helplessness has been applied to different situations, such as mental illness or abusive situations, but it can also be useful in an organizational setting. One aspect in which this concept applies is customer service, which is important in Stage Three of the loop but also important throughout the entire loop.

Consider a customer who is calling a company's help line. They dial the number, wait for an hour on the line, and are directed to someone who doesn't know their problem, or barely even speaks their language. The rep tells them they need to be transferred, but the call is disconnected. I'm willing to bet that almost everyone reading this has experienced something similar.

They call again and repeat the cycle. They try once more, and get bounced around from representative to representative until they get tired and finally hang up. Next time the customer has a problem, it's likely that they will not try calling again because they've already learned that's it's useless. They will have developed a learned helplessness concerning this company, and this experience is usually a frustrating one. It makes the individual feel helpless and hopeless—not the customer experience most customer-centric companies aim for.

Learned helplessness reflects physical processes in the brain that influence the entire body. The body has an underlying infrastructure that represents the fight/surrender dynamic. The autonomic nervous system is divided into the sympathetic branch and the parasympathetic branch The sympathetic branch is responsible for the activation of the fight/flight response that sends out adrenaline and hormones, and pumps blood away from the organs to the muscles; in short, it is energizing you and giving you the resources to fight. The parasympathetic branch does the opposite and underpins helplessness and depression. We fight for control but can, if the struggle gets too difficult, give it up.

At a neurological level, the brain decides it's not worth exerting any more energy and goes into conservation mode. Most animals have a coping strategy where they "play dead" in response to danger, a tactic that requires very little energy. The accompanying thought in humans when they do the same thing outside of a life-threatening situation is some variation of "I can't be bothered with this anymore." In the case of real threat, we will justify playing dead as a tactic to trick the enemy into believing we are no longer a threat or are indeed dead. In some ways, the angry or frustrated customer who is in fight or flight mode is easier to deal with than the one who has just given up. The one who has given up is no longer engaging you and is probably lost forever. They aren't just *playing* dead; they have left your world.

By now, it shouldn't be a secret that customer service plays an important role throughout the entire loyalty loop. The major difference, of course, is that your customers aren't dogs! (At least I don't think so.) Customers, unlike dogs, do have the opportunity to find a way out of the box. It's easier than ever before to find a new insurance agent, sell your car and get another, or find another provider. The same goes for complex B2B companies. There's more competition than ever before, and it's easier and faster than ever to shop the competition. Time and time again, this is where the breakdown occurs.

As you'll see in a moment, when there's very little competition, some companies can get away with having really bad service. It's sad for consumers who lie down like helpless dogs, but it represents the greatest opportunity to go from good to exceptional rather quickly.

Customer service is an incredibly misunderstood area of focus for most businesses. I have a strong reason to believe most experts, gurus, authors, and consultants are incredibly misguided as well when it comes to speaking and writing about these topics.

For example, they tell us things like how important it is to say "thank you." You already know that. Thankfully for you, I'm not one of them. But I'm incredibly dismayed whenever I hear a so-called customer service expert speak to an audience only to offer nothing more than basic platitudes about being nicer to the customers in general. In theory, it makes a lot of sense, but most people in business do a decent enough job at mustering up a simple thank-you. This has less to do with acknowledgments and more to do with maintaining a congruent experience all the way through.

As for the others, they seem to get by through sharing stories of companies who have done it right. For example, there were some 4,000+ books on Amazon that directly referenced Zappos as one of the more important customer service organizations on the planet. Most of them simply share collections of outrageous stories and examples of experiences and service-related moments where a company did something (somewhat) exceptional. For example, if I hear the story of the Ritz Carlton and the kid's stuffed animal from a speaker one more time, I'm going to lose it![3] Thankfully, I'm going to try not to do either of those things here. Instead, let's look at the science of customer service, which will allow your organization to thrive when it comes to providing a remarkable customer experience.

As I think about the concept of learned helplessness, I am reminded of some of the major players in the Canadian wireless industry. The service is just remarkably bad, and they get away with it. There's an oligopoly in Canada, and a few companies are profiting handsomely, but the service is just terrible. They treat customers poorly; they charge incredibly high prices, but there's not much we can do, so we lie down like helpless dogs. There's no customer loyalty. A quick Google search for some of the names of Canadian wireless companies yield hundreds of thousands of results from unhappy customers. Customers are stressed and frustrated, but there's not much they can do until someday maybe there is something they can do about it.

The best thing for you and your company is to realize "wow" and "remarkable" service aren't that difficult to achieve. That's your opportunity! The difference is that you can provide it and not just say it. Will you take it? Many companies have recognized that the times have changed, and if they keep shocking dogs, they're going to find themselves with no dogs left to shock. Below is one example.

Delight or Die

Gary Friedman is the CEO of Restoration Hardware, the high-end furniture retailer with revenues north of $500 million per year. In early 2016, Friedman issued a scathing memo to employees and told them to either DELIGHT the customer or find a new job.[4] The memo was fascinating in that Friedman explained the company was busy worrying about everything but the customer. Sound familiar? By this point in the book, it shouldn't.

He used the analogy of a burning building to say everyone seemed so interested in figuring out both how and why the building was on fire, or how to put out the fire, but not a single person was asking about the customers inside the burning building. In an interview with Bloomberg, Friedman said, "No one was focused on the people in the building, who were on fire. Their clothes were burning, and many of them dying. We have let customers die."

We have let customer die. Wow.

The company was in serious trouble. Aside from the fact that the company sells high-end furniture and has dozens of web pages dedicated to selling $17 light bulbs (yes, that's one light bulb for $17), the company was losing customers, revenue, and stock value. The stock dropped by over 26 percent just days before Friedman issued the memo. Friedman finished up by saying the new goal was to delight. The memo read: "We need a MASSIVE

CHANGE IN OUR CULTURE AND ATTITUDE RIGHT NOW...THE GOAL IS DELIGHT."

I don't know about you, but I've been hearing this word "delight" tossed around customer service circles for a while now.

Why is this concept of delight so important? I believe one of the reasons why is that we've been bombarded with the message that "customer satisfaction" is number one. It's one of the essential things companies must deliver to the customer. The trouble, however, is that allowing the customer to leave merely satisfied is never enough. The goal must be to go beyond satisfaction, and Restoration Hardware is recognizing this after years of continuous profit decline. Satisfaction is never enough, and I'm not sure sprinkled moments of delight are enough either, but done right, you have the opportunity to create memories that stick.

In the following pages, I'd like to introduce one of the most powerful things you can do in Stage Three to create distinct memories of doing business with your organization that stick.

I call them Remarkable Moments.

Remarkable Moments are the moments during the third stage of the loyalty loop that leave an indelible imprint in the customer's mind, one which they'll have no trouble recalling and explaining to friends and family— one that leaves them something specific and memorable to rant and rave about.

Let me share a few examples of Remarkable Moments in action so you can begin to understand how to apply these to your business and the moments and memories you may be able to create.

The Bentley and the Butler

Last year during a short trip to San Francisco, my wife and I dined at the fabulous Michelin-starred Ame restaurant at the St. Regis Hotel. My mentor and business colleague, Dr. Alan Weiss, was treating us to an incredible dinner.

Outside the hotel's lobby sat a gorgeous Bentley limo. The Bentley is offered as complimentary transportation for the hotel's guests. I've seen other high-end hotels offer cars like Rolls-Royces and Maseratis. I'm sure you have, too. A small boutique hotel in Cambridge, Ontario, called Langdon Hall recently offered guests the chance to drive a new Lexus SUV parked outside. The Trump Hotel recently took this a step further by providing guests access to the Trump helicopter to cruise the Scottish coastline.[5]

Imagine that! Stay at this hotel and you can fly in our private helicopter. Many organizations reserve these lavish perks for their top-spending customers. However, the companies that utilize this strategy most effectively are the ones who make these luxury perks available to most, if not all, of their clients. They use these perks to create memories within the customers' experience. These are Remarkable Moments, and they're available to all businesses of all types. I'll give you a few examples and some exercises to define and test your own.

Let's think through the economics of this here, because one of the main areas of concern is that you're spending money on customers who have already made it to the third stage. Why should you spend more to create Remarkable Moments?

The genius of this strategy is when you realize that the total amount they're paying to provide the Bentley equals about 3 percent per guest, for an experience that will make up 90 percent of their guests' memories, as well as the conversations they will have about their experience with the hotel. This is just one small example of how organizations are crafting experiences with emotional impact. They're carefully and strategically crafting memories that stick, and these are the things that people want to talk about. Seth Godin once said that the only definition of remarkable was to do something worth remarking about. This is the key to unlocking the power of Remarkable Moments.

And by the way, do you think that having these luxury experiences makes people less price sensitive? Of course, it does! This doesn't mean these lavish perks should be freely given to every customer, but companies should show every customer that the perks are available, as well as how to access them. You don't need to tie experiential rewards to a particular spend threshold or customer value. Instead, businesses must show customers a very easy path or way to access those perks.

A lot of companies try to use gimmicky promotions in exchange for their customer's continued business, in the hopes that it will create loyalty and positive associations. They use discounts and various promotions, hoping those promotions might drive a client back through their doors. The harsh truth is that those don't do much to influence customer loyalty. They're often forgotten before the transaction is finished.

The St. Regis Hotel, though, understands the power of customer experiences and Remarkable Moments. They know that nobody remembers—or ever talks about—saving $100 on a room discount, but everyone remembers—and wants to talk about—the Bentley.

Do not forget to consider fluidity amongst the first three stages of the Customer Loyalty Loop. This is just a small example of something done in the middle of the customer experience and the third stage, not the start or end of the customer experience, and yet it still generates a lasting memory. When used in sales and marketing before the sale, it creates the imagination of the experience to come, and the stories to be told. For example, after making my booking at Langdon Hall in Cambridge, Ontario, I received an e-mail in anticipation of my stay, inviting me to drive the Lexus during my stay. When I arrived at the hotel, there it was sitting out front.

These are just a few examples of Remarkable Moments in action. But where there's a Bentley, there's almost always a butler. Let's talk about a few more examples.

The Butler

Alfred was always there when Bruce Wayne needed something. Even in the depths of the bat cave, Alfred always seemed just to step out from the shadows ready to serve his crime-avenging leader. What if you could have your own Alfred?

Cruise lines, in particular, have embraced the concept of the butler. Dozens of the main cruise lines offer guests their very own private butler service. Usually reserved for passengers in suites, it is often sold as an upgraded service and sometimes as a surprise.

While the other guests are battling through the buffet lines, minding the sneeze guards, imagine for a moment, kicking your feet up, and your personal butler arriving at your suite's door with a bottle of champagne. He opens your patio doors, allowing the Florida breeze to rush in. As the ship sets sail, and all of your stresses would just float away.

The butler becomes the guest's personal concierge who knows how to get things done, even for the most discerning clients. This is remarkable! This is the type of thing I want to tell others about!

He handles the booking of daily excursions, reserves the best seats for ship's shows and makes dinner reservations for you, and fine-tunes the housekeeping services specific to the customer's liking, all while answering the guests' every question, concern, or request.

In essence, a modern ship's butler does all the hard work, raises the level of luxury a notch, and plays the perfect host, freeing those lucky passengers to enjoy a cruise to its fullest. Surely it must be expensive for a ship to offer such a service? There's no way most companies could offer such an extreme, lavish perk, right? Surely not your company.

Well, here's how the math and economics might work in this example. For each massive ship, the cruise line would likely have a small team of butlers, each of which would handle a small block of rooms and a certain number of guests.

At first, the experience might seem a bit incongruent with the expectations of the cruise. For many of us, the thought of cruises is not always one of luxury. We think of busy ships and cramped rooms jammed together. We regularly turn on the evening news to see another ship stricken with ill passengers. We've all heard horror stories. The butler, however, becomes a memorable experience and a Remarkable Moment. But how can a cruise ship afford to provide such remarkable service? There's no way your business could provide an experience of equivalent value, right? Well, let's do the math. Let's imagine for a moment the butler is paid $80,000 a year from the company. He's required to do approximately 25 cruises per year, and for each cruise he's provides his services to 12 rooms. For a little more than $250 per room, the cruise line has provided a fantastic perk with a tiny price tag. Now ask yourself, is the real purpose here to increase profits and generate more revenues? Partially. We can assure the cost is being paid for by the consumer one way or another, but let's suppose it's not. What's inadvertently happening is that for almost no cost at all the cruise is implanting an indelible memory into the customer's mind. For next to nothing, the cruise ship is creating its word-of-mouth marketing.

On a popular cruise website, one author shares the following story:

> The best I ever had was "Papa" on *Crystal Serenity*. Papa never felt intrusive to us. He suggested dinner to us in our stateroom on a night when he knew he could provide us with a table for the verandah. He wheeled in the table and served every dish piping hot. When we later asked for some caviar to entertain one of the guest speakers in our stateroom, Papa brought us caviar, champagne, brie, fresh fruit, and ended it with red wine and chocolate-covered strawberries. Never have I been more spoiled. I will never forget that experience on *Crystal Serenity*.

She will never forget Papa. Is this sinking in yet?

The key point is that the cost of the butler is irrelevant. The butler is the thing people remember. The butler is the thing people go home and talk about. The butler fuels word of mouth. If a customer was spending $10,000 with your company, would you be willing to spend $250 on that customer to create an experience that's never forgotten, to create an experience that people can't stop talking about—ever? You would be foolish not to. What if a company could spend considerably less, and create an experience with equal impact? It's not a question of *if* your company can do it, it's merely a question of what you will do to create the Remarkable Moments.

Remarkable Moments are the unique, fascinating experiences that allow a company to stand out from their competition. Sometimes these are high-value items, but the real key to Remarkable Moments is they create an emotional connection, and most importantly, a story that your customers want to tell others.

Many marketers espouse the idea of random moments of surprise and delight. I'm suggesting we take the concept of surprise and delight to another level, but it's shocking how many companies do this poorly. The most beautiful thing about this strategy is that just being good and better puts you way ahead of the competition. One of the core learnings of Stage Three is that it's up to you to define and create your company's Remarkable Moments. You can define the type of word of mouth your best customers spread about you. You can let word of mouth happen passively, or you can create it yourself.

How can you create your Remarkable Moments?

Action Step: Create Remarkable Moments

1) Write down the best and most memorable experience you've ever had with a business. Perhaps you're going to mention a company that is known for exceptional customer service. Companies like Disney, Nordstrom, Apple, and Amazon are routinely the ones that come to mind. But maybe you have a more interesting example. Ask yourself, what made that experience so remarkable? What were the specific things that made it memorable and created a lasting impression? What can you do in your business to create memorable moments across the entire experience?

2) Develop your Remarkable Moments. Brainstorm and have fun with this one. I want you to think about Remarkable Moments from Stage Three. What could you test that would positively shock your customers? What level of service could you deliver that would not believe is part of your standard process? For example, could you create a lavish perk reserved exclusively for your customers? Could you embrace the Zappos or Nordstrom ways and accept (almost) all return requests? Think outside the box and get creative. Remember nobody cares about the hotel room, but everyone talks about the Bentley and the butler. What's your Bentley? Who's your butler?

3) Test a Remarkable Moment. Remember the key Remarkable Moments. These businesses have carefully thought through the one single thing that's going to make your customer pick up the phone, call someone else, and say, "you won't believe what just happened at..." Remarkable Moments can be negative too, so why not control them?

Consider a few more examples.

When guests arrive at the Las Ventanas al Paraiso in San José del Cabo, Mexico, they are instantly whisked away to the spa's tranquil solarium, where they enjoy a surprise 10-minute neck and foot massage that releases any stress and worry from their flights and prepares them for a relaxing and rejuvenating stay in paradise.[6] Now that's a prime example of starting the customer experience right! On top of that, you're offering something guests are surely going to talk about. Remarkable Moments are exactly like they sound: moments worth making remarks about! If you want word of mouth, you often need to create the marketing to go with it.

Or how about the Viceroy Riviera Maya Hotel, also in Mexico, where a few minutes after checking in, the soap concierge arrives in your room to provide some informative information the different types of soaps available. The concierge explains the scents and the benefits of each soap. After that, the guest makes a selection, and personalized bars of soap are provided to each guest. Soap concierge. Remarkable Moments are just one part of the customer experience that you embrace in your business. Let's switch gears and talk about another important aspect of the science of customer experience—and that's the appeal to the customer's senses.

Let the Incense Burn

Love him or hate him, Donald Trump's hotels are second to none. While I'm not a fan of the way that Trump uses divisive language in the political arena, I am a huge fan of the attention to detail and experiences that are created at the hotels that brand his name (most of which are privately owned and operated without his direct involvement). I've stayed at a few of them, and when you enter from outside, you're usually suddenly thrust into a dimly lit lobby where the smell of incense burns, leaving an incredible aroma of eucalyptus through the air. The doorman quickly grabs your bags and sends them off to your room. After greeting you, the front desk clerk takes your credit card and then hands you a silver platter with a scented hot towel for wiping your hands and feet. Next, you're taken to your room where you're given a tour of the room, shown how the controls for lighting and window shades work, are introduced to the pillow menu, and a few other neat perks.

Why go to all this trouble with the customer experience? I mean, I've already decided to stay there, so why do all these extras? I'm beyond Stage Two of the Customer Loyalty Loop and well into Stage Three. Well, it turns out there are quite a few reasons to do this, and in this section, we'll look at the atmosphere and feeling your prospects and customers have when entering your business, or visiting your website. More important, we'll discuss ways in which you can utilize this powerful concept to have your customers spend even more money with your business.

In 2011, a study found that the more relaxed you are when entering a business, the more money you're likely to spend. As I think back to my stay at a number of Trump's properties, it's evident that while the service is incredibly warm and attentive, it's obvious that the entire guest experience has been carefully considered, from the moment we arrive, to the moment we make it to our rooms, to the moment we leave the property. It's as if the experience has been choreographed, where whimsical ballet dancers know when and where to hit their marks at which part of the experience.

This is the type of thing my clients are continuously thinking about. In this case, though, it was the way the experience started that left an impression on me.

Here are some key questions to consider:

1. How do your customers feel the moment they walk into your business or visit your online store?
2. Are customers always quickly greeted and welcomed?
3. Is the atmosphere of your business calming, or overwhelming, stressful, and busy?
4. Can my customer quickly find what she is looking for or do we present ourselves like a disheveled, messy closet?

Have you ever been to an Apple store? Most Apple stores I've been to are almost always completely jammed with people. It doesn't matter what time of day it is.

They're usually just full of people enjoying the opportunity to play with Apple's latest product. The one thing I've noticed, however, is that almost every Apple store has one or two people who immediately try to speak to every customer that comes in. They can quickly reduce the levels of stress by simply greeting the customer and sending them in the right direction. Contrast this to a large home improvement warehouse where you're looking for something as simple as light bulbs, and there's no help in sight. The store is overwhelming, and you're unable to find anyone to help you. Which experience is more pleasant? Almost all of us have been through both scenarios.

Traditional efforts suggest we need to provide more materials, more features, and more benefits, but by using the Customer Loyalty Loop, we can create experiences with impact by stimulating the mind and the senses.

Unbox This

There's a phenomenon happening on YouTube. People are making millions of dollars each year unboxing products and showing them off. According to Martin Lindstrom in his fantastic book *Buyology*,[7] the online unboxing craze began when a kid named Nick Baily filmed himself unboxing his brand-new Nintendo Wii. Lindstrom writes that the video had received over 70,000 views in just a few short hours. In his book, Lindstrom explains why unboxing has taken off as an Internet sensation. He attributes the desire to watch others unbox to mirror neurons. These are neurons inside our brains that, in laymen's terms, cause us to mirror other people's behaviors.

My children likely find joy in watching the excitement in the other kids unwrap their treats, and as Lindstrom explains, mirror neurons are the reason why we smile when we see others smile, and we wince when we see others in pain. It's the reason laughter is contagious. But beyond that, unboxing is a massively underestimated part of the customer's experience.

I think many of us would agree that this phenomenon started with Apple, who seemed to care as much about the packaging for its latest gadget as the products themselves. My children are particularly fond of the people who unbox chocolate Kinder Eggs and then put together the toys inside. How does unboxing fit into the Customer Loyalty Loop, and how can you best understand the ramifications of this? It fits in just the same as everything else fits in. Unboxing a product is part of the customer experience. This section is relevant to those in retail or who deliver physical products, but it is equally valuable to those who wish to perk customers with unexpected gifts or bonuses.

When a prospect has made the decision to convert and become a customer, if you've done things right up until now, then the customer should not feel a lot of buyer's remorse or anxiety about the decision. Instead, the buyer should be excited and eagerly anticipating the product's delivery. I still get excited when I get a new iPhone or a MacBook Pro. Apple has paid such careful attention to this part of the experience, and you're foolish not to treat it as such. Think about it this way: getting the product on your doorstep is part of the experience. Opening the package once it's inside your house is also part of the experience. Almost everyone has ordered a product only to be immensely disappointed once it arrives. Perhaps the box is damaged, or it's packaged poorly. Either way, we're left with a feeling of, "I spent all that money, and this is all I got!?" Or it's impossible to get it out of the packaging, which means that on the arrival of the package the customer is feeling total frustration rather than anticipated pleasure.

What products do you ship?

What items do you deliver to customers and clients?

Think about proposal or quote delivery, for example. Many companies e-mail these as quickly as they can. The more we can quote, the more we can close the typical mindset. But are you giving away undue and easily earned value in the mind of the potential customer by not couriering your proposal or a quote? When I work with clients, this is part of standard policy. I will typically ask the prospective client how they would like to receive the proposal. If they say they would prefer e-mail, I'll do that, but then I'll also send two signed copies via FedEx—one for them and one for me, but in reality, it's just another opportunity for me to give some value and treat this as part of the process of the overall customer experience.

If you're a retailer who physically ships products to customers, what can you do to add additional value to this part of the experience? Think about the entire experience as mentioned above. From getting the package, to opening the package, are your products carefully packaged? Is there joy in opening your package, or do you ship them as quickly and as cheaply as possible? If so, are you also giving away easily earned value? What little extras can you put into your packaging? Sometimes this is referred to as box candy.

Start thinking about every part of doing business with your company as an experience *for* the customer, and an experience to be *had* by the customer. Nearly all of this is about the emotional feelings your experiences create. Remember the old sales adage that "logic makes people think, but their emotions make them act." The entire customer experience is about the feelings and emotions you invoke in your customer's mind. Don't waste such a precious opportunity.

I think about Casper.com,[8] the company that disrupted the mattress industry selling over $75 million in mattresses in 2015. I can't think of a worse customer experience than buying a mattress. For years, we were expected to visit a store and spend 30 seconds to 5 minutes laying on a mattress. We were then asked to choose one, and days later a large moving truck would show up to deliver your mattress. The truck's drivers (no offense to them) were often gruff, burly guys just looking to unload the truck and punch out for the day. You had to ask them to take their shoes off, which was awkward, but they relented. The mattress was delivered into your bedroom, and three weeks later you woke to the realization that you bought a terrible mattress, your back was aching, and there was almost no easy way to return the product. Then, along comes Casper, who claims they've perfected the mattress. They're so sure, that they offer you the ability to try the mattress risk-free, in your home, for 100 days. We'll talk more about the psychology of guarantees and risk-reversal later, but Casper says, "Try it for 100 days, and if you're not convinced, call us and we'll pick up the mattress." The mattress is ordered online and within 5–7 days a great-looking blue box arrives at your door. You look at the box and say to yourself, surely there can't be a mattress in there. The box is a rectangle about the size of the small bar fridge you had in college. It's exciting. And then you lift the top of the box open to find a small plastic razor and some clever instructions that tell you to slide the mattress out of the box and only slice open the plastic when the mattress is in the room you'll use it in. The whole time, the customer is experiencing something that has never, in the history of buying, been exciting before—buying a mattress. Next, you slice open the plastic, and slowly the mattress expands to full size. It's really like magic, or perhaps a bit like a teenage boy finally getting his chance to dance with the head cheerleader.

Casper encourages you to sleep on it, to jump on it, to play on it, and to make sure it's perfect for you. If not, you're welcome to call them anytime in the first 100 days and request a refund. They promise to make that part of the experience as stress-free as possible. And what they do is pretty remarkable. They call the local Goodwill or Salvation Army to pick up the mattress, and it's donated to a local group in need. That's pretty amazing if you ask me. Meanwhile, your entire amount paid is refunded back to your credit card. It's an incredible customer experience and one that has earned the company over $75 million in revenue in just a few short years of business. Not too shabby if you ask me.

Here are a few questions to consider:

How much attention are you paying to the delivery of your products and services?

What could you do to make this part of the experience more fulfilling and engaging for the customer?

Where are you looking for shortcuts when you could be offering additional value?

When you think of unboxing, don't just think of products, think of the entire unboxing of your experience. What's the first moment like when the customer checks into the hotel? Are they whisked off to a massage? Is there a fruit basket and handwritten note waiting in the room?

I know a company that sells a massive piece of machinery; the equipment can cost upwards to $1 million a unit.

Paying careful attention to the unboxing and delivery of your products and services could add millions of additional revenue to your bottom line. Oh, and before I forget, the Casper mattress is glorious, and hand's down the best mattress I've ever slept on.

Maximizing Customer Value
During the Experience
. . . .

When it comes to creating frenzied buying behavior in the retail sector, we have to look no further than the iconic blue building with the giant yellow block-lettered sign that reads IKEA. It turns out that Ikea isn't just remarkably clever when it comes to fitting an entire bedroom into three small boxes that fit into a Mini Cooper, but they've also mastered the art of using psychology to get us to buy, buy more, and buy again.

In 2011, on the popular site called Reddit, an Ikea employee started a thread known as an iAMA (Reddit terminology for I Am A..., and Ask Me Anything). In response to one question, he made reference to sections of the store known as "Open the Wallet" sections.[9] This represents the cacophony of small, relatively cheap items that are scattered all over the popular Swedish store with the intent on making us open our wallets. If you've been to an Ikea store before, then you've seen them all over. For example, on a recent trip to an Ikea store, I noted a large yellow bin filled with small aluminum pots for $4.95 each. Another stairwell contained candle holders and tea lights, and little green stools for children to stand on in the bathroom. All three of these items came home with us.

What is it about these items that cause customers to open their wallets, and how can you do the same if your business is lacking a 300,000-square-foot retail operation? It's quite simple, and a few powerful psychological things are going on. First, many of these items are found as you first enter the store, whether they're in a stairway or bins next to the front entrance. Ikea knows that once you commit to buying, you are more likely to buy again. They're taking advantage of recency and frequency, which we'll talk about in the next stage. They're also taking advantage of the commitment principle, which suggests you're more likely to follow through on something after you've committed to it. Second, the items are all priced low enough but seem practical enough that if you've already spent this much, you might as well throw this in the cart. Who doesn't need a green plastic toilet brush for 99 cents? Third, the items are placed repetitively throughout the store. You might not need a green plastic toilet brush yet, but after the third or fourth time seeing it, you might be convinced. Here are a few questions to consider: What are you doing throughout the third stage that creates opportunities to increase customer value? Without having loads of obnoxious upsells peppered throughout your business, how can you create no-brainer opportunities for the customer to buy, and buy again? That's a question worth asking in during the third stage.

Peak-End Rule and the
Psychology of Lasting Impressions

It is worth revisiting the way the mind works at this point to highlight the importance of creating the right experience. The binary brain would have us believe that there is a clear distinction between emotions and thoughts. One is about feelings, the other rationality. In the same way that economics had a view of the rational man who would always make the best financial decisions based on logical analysis, far too much emphasis has been placed on rationality in purchasing decisions and consumer behavior. Psychologist Daniel Kahneman won the Nobel Prize in economics by debunking the rational economic man myth. As you think about this dynamic between emotions and thought, it is easy to believe that emotions override logic or vice-versa, in a sort of wrestling match between different parts of the brain. However, there is the view in some quarters that rather than being opposites, emotions and thoughts are interdependent and that you can't have one without the other. This is the view of Antonio Damasio, an esteemed neurologist and author of the best-selling book *Descartes' Error: Emotion, Reason, and the Human Brain*.[10] Part of the evidence for this view comes from cases where people have suffered neurological damage that impacts the emotional areas of the brain. Rather than turning into logical superstars who are freed from the tyranny of emotions, such people can't make a decision. The implication, therefore, is that thought requires some emotional input. We certainly know from Elizabeth Loftus' work, mentioned earlier, that the level of emotion influences perception and memory. So emotion and the experience are king because they have a major impact on memory, perception, and thought. Moreover, the value of this experience does not exist on a continuum. Rather, the more extreme the experience, the more it is overvalued and the less it is influenced by rationality. So just as we have incongruences negatively impacting perceptions, congruency with very positive expectations will turn a customer into a loyal and ardent supporter.

If emotional valence is important in influencing, if not determining, thoughts then obviously a peak experience is the key to converting a customer into a fan. But what's the opposite of a peak experience? One assumes that a negative emotional experience is the opposite of a peak experience. If you aggravate a customer so that she is angry and frustrated with you, you are obviously at serious risk of losing her as a customer. However, the experience and behavior of a psychologist friend of mine might have some bearing on this issue.

How do you get excellent service at a restaurant? My friend used what he called "post-conflict compensation"—I told you he was a psychologist—to get his great service. Here's what he would do: When the server first came over to greet him, my friend expressed surly frustration at some aspect of the early dining experience. He might have complained about a spot on the tablecloth or dirty cutlery, just something that would create some conflict. Typically, the server would attend, often grudgingly, to the complaint. Then when the server came back again, my friend would apologize, often praising the server for behaving so professionally. Often he found the attention he got after that was sublime. The point is that even negative emotions can be turned into great experiences, sometimes precisely because they started out negative and then were reversed. Being moved from a negative emotional state to a positive one is a very motivating and rewarding experience, especially in an interaction or a relationship. It is how you can go from bad to exceptional pretty quickly. Think about the drive for "make-up sex." It's the same mechanism, where reversing negativity results in a disproportionate sense of closeness. I'll talk more about this in Sage Four.

So we have considered experiences at both ends of the emotional spectrum. What can we say about experiences that have very little associated emotion? The customer who has little or no emotional experience when dealing with you is not engaged with you as a brand or business, or with your process. They don't think especially highly of you or badly about you. That's the problem: they don't think about you at all—well, not in any meaningful way. They are the customers that can, and do, go elsewhere. They are not committed or loyal to you.

Take a look at how the traditional customer journey compares to the loyalty loop (see Figure 5.1). The traditional customer experience starts with attention, but then fades off quickly. Because resistance has not been removed, there's a negative drip immediately after the sale. The experience is erratic and usually tapers off. Even a decent experience with a company is not often remembered that well because the company has gone back to chasing new customers. Contrast this to the loyalty loop, which maintains a strong start and continues to a point of happily ever after. In the loyalty loop, customer happiness and emotional engagement starts at a much higher level and is maintained throughout. The typical customer experience is a roller coaster of peaks and valleys, and that's why so many companies fail to deliver a memorable and remarkable customer experience.

Figure 5.1: The Traditional Customer Experience vs. the Loyalty Loop Experience

Earlier in the book, we discussed the importance of how experiences end as having a dramatic impact on the likelihood that the customer is willing to reenter the relationship with your business and experience it again. You might guess from the above that it is your last experience that counts, because that is the one that is likely to be most prominent in your memory. If you like, it's where you left off in your relationship. This raises one of the more widely used psychology findings known as the peak-end rule. It is important for us to remember and recognize how the main customer experience ends, and what we can do to set the foundation for the fourth stage.

Early on we talked about Daniel Kahneman's findings with the way people experience—the experiencing self and the remembering self. Kahneman is one of the central figures in proposing the peak-end rule theory. In a nutshell, the peak-end rule is a psychological finding that suggests people judge experiences not based on the entire experience, but how it was at its peak and how it was when it ended. An example we gave earlier on suggests that even a fantastic seven-day stay at a hotel can be ruined by a bad experience on checkout. A great restaurant experience can be ruined by an argument over the bill with the waitstaff. Or, as in the case of my psychologist friend, a bad experience can be turned into a great one. Are your experiences ending as positively as they should be? In Stage Three, we need to consider how the experience ends and how we can prime our customer for additional buying experiences to come. The main lesson in this section is you can't be foolish and unaware about how the experience ends.

- How are the customers acknowledged and thanked when they leave?
- If required, how is the final invoice presented?
- In a B2B scenario, is there a final walk-through or project ending?
- In a consulting arrangement, is there an official project disengagement meeting?
- How can you make the endings as positive as possible, or are you just leaving them to change?

Don't miss this fabulous opportunity to create a memory that lingers.

At first, many people in business assume once they've got the customer, the hard work is done. Now, we've effectively looked at all the important parts of the customer journey during the delivery of our products and services. It's at this point that another large segment of people in business assume the work is done. They assume that if they've done a good job, the customer will likely return. If they've pleased the customer, then the customer will likely tell others. If they've delighted the customer and created Remarkable Moments, the customer is likely to go home and shout from the rooftops. They assume all of this happens without any work, effort, or process. And that's an entirely false assumption. When working with clients, I'm always asking about follow-up process, and almost everyone looks at me with blank stares—sad but true. When we start to implement even a small chunk of what I often have to argue tooth and nail to get implemented, the results are mind-boggling. Let's look at the final stage now and see how your business matches up.

The Evergreen Experience Audit

Earlier in the book, I mentioned a process I engage in with a number of my clients called the Evergreen Experience Audit. The minimum fee to engage in this process with my company is $17,500—that's the minimum—and it always generates a demonstrable ROI, but I'm going to give it to you here in this book that likely cost you less than $20. If you decide you want us to come help with the audit, we'd be more than happy to do that. The Evergreen Experience Audit is a five-step process designed to look at the whole customer experience regardless of the type of business or industry you're in. One of the common buzz phrases used in the customer experience world is "touch points." Touch points are all the times you engage with clients throughout each stage of the loop. In some cases, you might have only one or two touch points through each stage. The bigger and more sophisticated a company gets, the more touch points they have. There are touch points in Stage One in marketing, touch points in the sales process in Stage Two, perhaps multiple touch points with your front-facing staff in Stage Three, and additional touch points as you continue to follow up with the customer. As we've discussed throughout the book, even one poor touch point can paint a negative picture of all the positive ones. The goal of the experience audit is maintaining congruency throughout all touch points. That's not always easy—experience expectations about what happens during each stage and through the various touch points can be vastly different amongst the executive suite, management, front-facing staff, and even your customers.

Using the process that I'm going to share with you now, we close the gap between what your customers expect and what's actually delivered; we also close the gap between the differing expectations amongst your people. I can't stress enough how important it is to do this on a regular basis. It's not difficult; in fact, you won't believe how easy it is. The reason it's powerful to have an outside party do this is because you and your team are biased. The confirmation bias creeps in to make us feel we're doing things right. The real results and power come from having someone with the right expertise to not pull any punches. When I do this, I've already been paid. I'm not working with clients to make friends. I'm there to discomfit and create change. Sometimes this doesn't always work out. I had a client that hired me to do a meeting with their salespeople. There were 80 of them from around the globe who gathered for a one-day sales meeting. Almost every time I speak, there's extensive predatory work on my end. I talked to some of the salespeople. I talked to their customers. I talked to management and executives. And what I found were wildly different expectations about the whole customer experience. I warned my buyer that I wasn't going to come down easy, but perhaps say things that might make people uncomfortable. Sure enough, that's exactly what happened. While some of the attendees said the workshop was "enlightening" and "fascinating" and "some of the most valuable work we've ever engaged in," others didn't feel this way. As I explained to my buyer, "There are always people discomfited by change and/or who seek to critique, but that's not my concern." If you don't hire someone like me to help you engage in a process like this, consider engaging your own customers to help, or having other outsiders do it for you.

Action Step: Evergreen Experience Audit

Step 1: Process Diagnosis

The first step involves looking at the customer journey as it pertains to your business and simply having a discussion about it. If you're a large organization and have multiple divisions, this step just starts with a conversion. Talk about the customer experience as a whole using each stage as a guidebook. For example, what customer touch points are happening in the early marketing stages—how about when a lead raises her hand, or how about once they finally sign on the dotted line. What about after the sale? You get the idea. In Step 1, we're simply surveying the landscape to get an understanding of what's happening at each stage. You can use some of the other Action Steps to help you diagnose the experience.

Step 2: Employee Understandings

In the second step, you want to test your employees. There's no pass or fail here. Well, that's not true. You can fail, and perhaps fail miserably. I've done this part of the process with teams all within the same department only to find wildly different expectations and understandings about what was happening and what was expected of them. In this step, you want to have everyone write out all the customer touch points that they believe are happening and are expected of them. Ask them to map it.

Step 3: Customer Stories

In the third step, you want to talk to your customers. I don't mean lousy and somewhat useless surveys like the one-question NPS survey. Talk to them. Ask them to tell you about their experiences. Read your recent reviews and stories from customers. If someone's experience sounds awful, reach out and learn exactly why they were upset. Interview your customers and record their experience. Share these with the appropriate teams. When we do this to our clients, we talk to perhaps dozens of customers across the entire customer experience, from Stages One through Four, to see how the customers were truly feeling throughout each experience with your company.

Step 4: Undercover Boss

The hit television show *Undercover Boss* always makes me laugh because it shows just how complacent owners and executives have become. I always love the scene where the CEO returns to the boardroom and they're all just shocked at what the boss experienced. Could they really have been that surprised with what they learned? I doubt it. Most of the time, I do a quick Google search and find dozens of the horror stories shared by their customers.

In my experience, CEOs and business owners often have very little idea with what's actually happening in their companies on a day-to-day basis. In this part of the process, you want to experience the process from the eyes and ears of the customer at each stage in the process. For example, you want to answer the phones. You want to work on the front lines. You want to go visit the shop floor. You want to run the front desk or the service counter for a day. You get the idea. There's no need to wear silly costumes.

Step 5: The Hierarchy of Horrors

Take your learnings from the previous four steps and create a Hierarchy of Horrors.

The Hierarchy of Horrors is a process I learned from Michael Basch, who was one of the founding executives at FedEx. In his book titled *Customer Culture: How FedEx and Other Great Companies Put the Customer First Every Day*, Basch offered the Hierarchy of Horrors. In my opinion, this is a fantastic process to take what you've learned in the first four steps of the Evergreen Experience Audit and create an action plan around them. When I'm engaged in the audit with a client, we use a slightly different process but the essence is the same.

There are four simple steps to the Hierarchy of Horrors:

1. List the eight worst places where you're messing up with your customers.
2. Measure the mistakes over the next 30 days. FedEx measured things like missed deliveries, damaged packages, and so on.

3. Add up the results and categorize your horrors from bad to worst.
4. Work backwards by improving areas you're the worst in measure.

Work on one area at a time. When you've made significant improvements in that area, move on to the next.

Step 6: Every 90 Days

Schedule at least one day every 90 days that you'll spend getting in touch with your customers and employees. If your salespeople meet customers on site, spend a day traveling with them to meet prospective customers. If you have a customer service line, spend an entire day answering the phones and talking to customers. Sit in with other reps to see how calls are answered and handled.

I'm giving you a brief understanding of the process, and you can certainly engage in this type of experience audit yourself. But if you're interesting in a more thorough, in-depth look at the experience at your company, or across multiple locations (perhaps hundreds or even thousands of locations) and different divisions with multiple service offerings and multiple customer experiences, feel free to get in touch.

6. Stage Four: Happily Ever After

If you create a great experience, people tell their friends, but you don't own the gas pedal on that. No attempt we've made to bribe our customers into telling more people or even inspire them into telling more people by making charitable contributions and other things, has ever given us a gas pedal on word of mouth referrals. The best gas pedal on word-of-mouth referrals is just a great experience.
—Gail Goodman, CEO of Constant Contact[1]

The customer who has recently finished a transaction with you is more likely to engage in a transaction with you again. This is the power of recency. And, the more frequently a customer engages in a transaction with you, the more likely they are to continue that behavior. This is the power of frequency. The entire loop and adopting a retention/loyalty-focused mind-set is about increasing a customer's frequency and willingness to engage in business activities with you again and again. In the business world, this is often referred to as the recency, frequency, monetary (RFM) value model. As we think back to previous stages of the book, the model makes sense on many fronts, primarily with how the customer is feeling at each stage of the process.

Back in the 20th century, German psychologist Hermann Ebbinghaus called a similar concept the serial position effect.[2] Analogous to the RFM model, the serial position effect deals with primacy and recency—primacy as it relates to the first stage of the loop and the ability to be preeminent in the customer's mind, and primacy as it relates to first impressions and so on. People are more likely to remember what happens at the beginning of an experience and the end of the experience, but they often forget the middles.

Ebbinghaus was his own research subject, committing himself to learning thousands of lists of apparently "nonsense" words that had been made up of two consonants and a vowel, like HEB. Despite the fact that these words were made up and had no meaning, subsequent research showed that people would try to associate the words to those they already knew and thus ascribe some sort of sense to them. Ebbinghaus was famous for identifying the forgetting curve, which plots the rate of loss of learned information. He found that the greatest decline occurred in the first 20 minutes and is significantly larger in the first hour. Ebbinghaus also described the learning curve in which most information is learned at the first attempt, and less information is learned after each repetition. Perhaps this explains the "first impression" effect—it's difficult to unlearn initial information or learning.

Ebbinghaus also identified the serial position effect, in which recency and primacy seemed to enhance learning. Ebbinghaus believed that the recency effect worked because the information was still in short-term memory. The primacy effect works because there is more time to rehearse and commit to long-term memory compared with items that come later in the list.

Another relevant concept that Ebbinghaus came up with is that of "savings." What he found was that even after he had forgotten a list, he could subsequently relearn it much faster than he did learning it the first time around. He assumed that even though he had consciously forgotten a list, it was still lurking in his subconscious and was quickly recruited when he was exposed to it again. His memory had been "jogged." This has real implications for the Customer Loyalty Loop. How you treat a customer isn't relevant just to their immediate experience, it is also likely to recruit similar past experiences that they have probably forgotten. Customers aren't likely to be going around constantly remembering the great customer support they received until they get it again. Of course, the same works for negative experiences. Every time you interact with a customer, you are likely to remind them of their past experiences with you, especially if they were more than neutral interactions.

Dropping the Customer Follow-Up Ball

In the Customer Loyalty Loop, recency is the crucial underpinning of your customer follow-up processes and procedures. The more recently someone has engaged in business with you, the more likely they are to be interested in what you have to say (or to do it again). Now here's a big distinction: the onus isn't on the customer to come back and be more "recent." It's not up to the customer to conduct transactions with you more frequently. Instead, the onus is on you, the business owner, the brand, to work to bring the customer back to buy, buy more, and buy again after that.

Most companies drop the ball in Stage Four because they've moved back to the thrill and excitement of finding new customers. It's backward thinking. If I do business with a company and then the first time I hear from them is six or eight months later, then they were likely better off not following up at all! It creates negative associations for many customers. But if I'm contacted 10 or 15 days after I do business with you with the right type of request or reach-out, then I'm more likely to do business with you again and react positively to whatever it is you send me. The memory of our experience is still fresh at this point. So ask yourself, how soon after the transaction ends are you making your next contact with a customer? The more recently they've done business with you, the more likely they are to respond and be interested. But it needs to be the right type of reach-out. Many go right for the jugular, hoping the positive word of mouth starts flowing after the first experience. To do that, they use something called Net Promoter Score. which I believe is a terrible tool for measuring customer loyalty.

Stop Measuring NPS

In 2003, Fred Reichheld, a partner at Bain & Company, introduced the Net Promoter Score.[3] NPS was introduced as a management tool that could help companies gauge and understand customer loyalty as it applied to revenue growth. The model was incredibly simple and became—and has remained—one of the most important tools for measuring customer loyalty over the past 10 years. Customers of a company were asked a single question, using a 0–10 scale: How likely is it you would recommend (insert brand/company) to a friend or colleague? This is the official NPS question. Respondents were then grouped into categories like:

- Promoters (score 9–10) are loyal enthusiasts who will keep buying and refer others, fueling growth.
- Passives (score 7–8) are satisfied but unenthusiastic customers who are vulnerable to competitive offerings.
- Detractors (score 0–6) are unhappy customers who can damage your brand and impede growth through negative word of mouth.

Subtracting the percentage of Detractors from the percentage of Promoters yields the Net Promoter Score, which can range from a low of −100 (if every customer is a Detractor) to a high of 100 (if every customer is a Promoter). NPS has long been hailed the ultimate customer loyalty measurement tool, but in my opinion it's a relatively useless tool. I have a slight suspicion it makes bigger brands and organizations feel good about their efforts because it takes an average look across all customers. If most are considered promoters, then they must be doing something right. If more are passive, then they know where to focus some efforts.

There are several things wrong with the NPS approach from a simply statistical perspective. There's the question of the reliability and validity of the standard questionnaire that asks customers to rate service on a linear scale. Reliability refers to whether someone will reliably give the same answer to the same question. If they don't, the questionnaire is useless. Validity refers to how well a tool measures what it intends to measure, and it depends on the questionnaire being reliable to begin with. For example, does the answer truly reflect the customer's views? Perhaps they just want to fill out the form and send it back as soon as possible and aren't concerned about accuracy. Perhaps the answer given just reflects the mood that the customer happens to be in at the time they complete the rating scale. The scale is also very subjective, and people vary in their criteria of service so that one person's 5 is another person's 9. This problem is mitigated a little when there are descriptions of the numbers on the scale (e.g., "A 10 means that service was perfect,"), but then *perfect* is a subjective judgment. So, what correlation is there between a customer's rating scale and the probability of them buying from you again? A rating scale is not the basis of a relationship. Completing a typical rating scale is not a peak experience; in fact, it's not much of an experience at all.

There may be ways of making a rating scale a bit more fun and more interactive, for example, by adding an animated character to guide you through the rating. Interactivity is the key, here. But while we might have fun and even some excitement interfacing with an animated character, for example, there is nothing like the right person-to-person interaction to create a bond, trust, and ultimately, loyalty. And that personal interaction has to be authentic.

How can you make your post-sales (that is after the customer's most recent purchase but also before his or her next purchase) communications memorable? Sending a standard form used by everyone else hardly makes you memorable. Asking the same questions in the same way that doesn't distinguish you from the competition hardly makes you memorable.

There are other reasons why NPS is relatively useless. Some of the big reasons should be obvious. For example, it doesn't matter how many promoters you might have based on the single survey question. Because unless you have referral programs and tools in place to encourage word of mouth, then it means nothing. In essence, by looking at averages, it misses out on looking at one-to-one perspective and experiences with a company as an opportunity to improvement. Even if 100 customers told a company their service was horrific and Johnny was a rotten account executive, they might not be willing to do anything about it, because overall NPS scores are still averaging on the high end. Johnny still continues to damage your company behind the scenes.

In 2016, in an interview with Bloomberg, Reichheld discussed how the single post-purchase follow-up survey has officially "jumped the shark" as companies merely bribe their customers by asking for 10s instead of using the survey as an opportunity to create improvement—or in this case, extend the loyalty loop.[4] The employees don't care what the customers have to say, so they bribe the customers to give top marks. Companies say things like "It would be really valuable for us if you gave us a 10." What good does that do to help you improve your customer's experience? Nothing. It's rather damaging because it signals to customers that "we don't truly care if you're happy or not. We only care if we get high marks." In larger companies, you have these huge investments into adhering to the NPS program, and then front-line employees bribing customers to give 10s. The scores end up as valuable as a bundle of Lehman Brothers stock.

The other huge issue, of course, is that the number means absolutely nothing unless you understand what's required after the sale to bring a customer back or to extend the loyalty loop and create the next desired action from your customer. Even with all the Remarkable Moments, great memories, and positive feelings you've created throughout the customer's experience, people eventually get back to real life. This means that your past customers aren't spending 24/7 thinking about the next time they'll do business with you. In fact, it's almost the opposite. They return to a normal life where kids get sick, cars break down, bills need to be paid, Ob-La-Di, Ob-La-Da life goes on. Who cares if they would score you a 10 on the NPS scale? The only thing that matters is *if* they will actually tell someone about you and they actually do it; *if* they actually come back and do business with you, and so on, and so on. There are a lot of ifs. And perhaps, most important, *if* your company is willing to make changes if your scores are poor. A lot of people in business have a hard time understanding that people aren't thinking about spending money with their businesses each and every waking moment of the day.

If you only ask one silly NPS question, how will you know where you're dropping the ball? How will you know where you need to improve and do a better job? How will you know where to invest your marketing dollars?

It's our job in Stage Four to have the right processes and procedures in place to ensure all of those things and more happen. The loyalty loop can be repeating for a single customer, and it also spirals to create new customers and new opportunities, but only when you have the right processes in place to make that happen. Consistency and familiarity are the keys to Stage Four and creating the right environment for word of mouth and referrals to happen. Just because my first experience is a good experience, does not necessarily mean I'm ready for a silly one-question survey about if I'm willing to refer. I'm likely not ready yet, and asking me at the wrong time can actually influence my memory of a great experience gone bad. Remember back to earlier chapters and the seemingly wonderful experiences ruined by a poor ending. I may be only willing to refer after my fifth or eighth purchase.

Oh, and the day before writing this, I got an NPS survey from a company that I haven't given a dime to in four years. I also continue to get their "customer-only" newsletters. This is a company that's doing north of $50 million a year revenue and has been on the Inc. 5000 list half a dozen times in the past eight years. Now you might be saying, "So what, Noah? They're doing annual revenue of over $50 million a year." Yeah, but they could be doing $125 million if they were doing things right. I bet they could. Is your business more about checking the boxes and less about generating meaningful results? And that's the key distinction here. Moreover, the request from the company I haven't done business with isn't just blatantly wrong; it's entirely inappropriate. I'm not a customer and haven't been in a long time. This is just one way so many companies are encouraging negative word of mouth. I was in a meeting once where a CEO found out his people weren't following up on quotes of about $30 million a year. He looked at his people and everyone sat in stunned silence. Finally, he said, "Here's what we're going to do! Every month we're going to have a big old' bonfire in the company parking lot. I'll give you all $250,000 of my money. At least this way we can toast marshmallows." Harsh example, but so true. Let's talk about how much follow-up, how often, and why it's important.

The 90–45 Rule

I was conducting a workshop with a B2B client when one of the attendees in the back of the room raised his hand. He said, "I've got a confession to make. Actually, it's more of a story." He told us a story about a job he was working on with a client. When the work was completed, this employee visited the client's site, a large restuarnat, to ensure everything was performed as expected. The job went remarkably well and the client was thrilled. He then said, "And that was the last I heard from them." So I asked him if he followed up. He said no. I asked the sales team if anyone else followed up. They said no. I asked the marketing people in the room if they followed up. They weren't sure either. Then he told us the rest of the story. He went to the client's restaurant for lunch one day. He arrived to find one of their main competitors working on another job. They didn't lose the business because of a poor customer experience or a customer service blunder. In fact, it was the total opposite. The Customer Loyalty Loop broke down in Stage Four because nobody followed up. Nobody maintained contact with the client. Nobody sent them anything valuable or got in touch to see how things were going. This was the *only* reason they lost the work. That's it.

Another client had a similar challenge. The products they sold were more expensive and the buying cycle was less frequent, but the CEO knew they weren't doing a good enough job developing and nurturing the relationships with their clients. With this client, we put a simple yet incredibly powerful tool into place called the **90–45 rule**. I began calling it the 90–45 rule because those were the specific dates that were important to this client when creating the rule.

The rule we put into place was simple. It said that *no* client who had ever spent a dime with this specific company was allowed to go more than 90 days without at least a 15-minute phone call, but preferably a 30-minute, in-person meeting with their specific sales rep.

Further to that, we took the top 10 percent of customers for each sales rep and adjusted the rule so that no customer could go 45 days without the same follow-up. How does this apply to your business? How often should you be following up and maintaining contact? The Customer Loyalty Loop requires proactive effort. You get out of the loop what you put into the loop. For your business it might be a 3–7 rule. For others, it might be entirely different. The point is to keep in contact! It's a horrible feeling showing up at a happy client's place of business only to find your best competitor doing your work. It's scary, but it's happening far more often than you think.

Here's a crucial component of the 90–45 rule: the 90–45 rule is about personal communication. The more frequently you communicate with customers in a way that adds value to them and their interests, the more revenue your company will generate. The key here is the communication is in their best interest and not your own self-interest. People smell ill-intent a mile away.

Action Step: Follow-Up Frequency

Determine the optimal communication frequency with your top customers, suppliers, partners, and others. Notice I didn't just say end customers. Think about your top partners and suppliers.

Determine the appropriate frequency for the right type of follow-up. What makes sense for your business? Is it 90–45? Is it 70–30? You have to determine what's right for your business.

Find a way to measure and track the activities to make sure they're actually happening. Some of my best clients have used a special tracking tool that my company has developed solely for these types of efforts (you'll learn more about this in the Pick-3 Process). The tool provides a reminder of which clients require which type of follow-up on which days.

1. Assign tasks and responsibilities. Everyone in your company should be taking part. This isn't just a process for the folks in sales. This is a job everyone should be doing. The CEO or VP of Marketing should be making calls to the likely peers at their suppliers, distributors, and partners.

2. Set up exception reporting. The reason most training and new initiatives like the 90–45 rule fail is because there's nobody to hold people accountable. In all the work I do with my clients,

we set up exception reporting. This means that if something isn't tracked, measured, or documented then it didn't happen. Further to that, managers, VPs, owners, and CEOs will receive regular reporting on the things that were supposed to happen, but didn't. It's up to them to ask *why not?*

3. How often can you routinely communicate on a more personal level with your customers? Brainstorm the ideas with your team.

I get a lot of pushback when I explain something as simple as the 90–45 rule. People say that their customers don't want to hear from them, or they are reluctant because such calls and "check-ins" feel awkward. But nine times of out 10, when I find customers leaving businesses to go to the competitors, I find a very flimsy sense of loyalty to certain companies; when we dig down to discover why, it becomes apparent that the other guys are showing up more often. Remember the definition of loyalty. Loyalty is about connection, and connection is about feeling. It's the feeling that I have a relationship with you, and you have a relationship with me. This is about maintaining an open, honest, friendly, and supportive relationship with your customers. Trust me, it's worth it. Everyone has to take part. Every single client that has implemented a simple 90–45 rule has handsomely profited handsomely. You could be next.

The Pick-3 Process
• •

The age of high tech often reduces our ability for high touch, but of course proper use of high tech can enable high touch in the most effective ways. One of the simplest yet most effective tools I've ever given my clients is what I call the **Pick-3 Process**. I was working with a large B2B manufacturing company where everything that could be going wrong was going wrong. They were losing clients and market share to their competitors, and sales weren't increasing either. The CEO had heard me speak and knew he needed to hire me to help. Instead of spending too much time explaining exactly what was happening, I'll keep it relatively simple: they weren't following up—at all. I was hired to help. What I loved about this company was that they weren't willing to allow one department to take the blame for the current state. Instead, the objective was to change the entire culture of the company to focus almost exclusively on following up, and the Pick-3 was born. Similar to the 90–45 rule, Pick-3 is about assigning specific loyalty loop–related tasks throughout the entire organization.

We do this through a simple tool designed to ensure the right things are happening consistently when they should be, and if they're not, then management is aware of it. We know the last time John at ABC Tire was contacted because it's in the system. Now you might be thinking this sounds a lot like a customer relationship management (CRM), like Salesforce or any of the dozens of other tools out there, but it's not because this is all about action and activity as it relates to deepening the relationships with our customers. Without going into too much detail on the system we provide many clients, it's not necessary to develop your own Pick-3 Process.

Build Your Pick-3 Process

Pick-3 is simple. Every day, you and your team each engage in three simple tasks related to the Customer Loyalty Loop. That's it. Three tasks, all of which should take no less than 15 minutes. Now you might be thinking, this seems pretty simplistic, but this is where you take advantage of the power of compound interest. When we get an entire division or an entire company engaged in these tasks, the results are incredible. If you really want to be a customer-centric company, this is how you do it. You can stop worrying about all that other stuff, because Pick-3 is about the rubber meeting the road in terms of actionable tasks designed to build and develop the relationships with your customers. So, we have tasks every single day, for everyone taking part. You then need to track that the tasks are being done every single day. And you rinse and repeat, and you add new tasks as you go. Think of a diagram like the one in Figure 6.1. This could be filled with dozens of different options for your people. The goal is to complete three tasks per day, per employee, that drive customer loyalty and customer satisfaction. Just imagine if thousands of these actions were being completed each day! Now that's what you call customer centricity.

Figure 6.1: Pick-3 Process

Here are a few examples.

Pick-3 Example Task 1: Call three of your highest-value clients in terms of revenue.

Pick three of your best customers and clients based on revenue and call them. Review their client record to understand the last time they purchased and what they purchased. Review the last time someone else spoke to them. Spend another 30 seconds conducting a quick

Google search to see if there's anything about them in the news. Make a note of the last time they purchased or anything newsworthy about them. Remember, this call is about putting the customer's interests ahead of yours. If you call them to pitch your latest offering, then you're doing it wrong.

Pick-3 Example Task 2: Send Three Handwritten Notes

Don't underestimate the power of the handwritten note. In our day and age of high tech, we've lost touch with low-tech, high-value follow-up that's meaningful and memorable. One company built a thriving business by sending 13,000 handwritten thank-you notes. I routinely send things to my top clients. I might send a small handwritten note with a newspaper article I've clipped that's relevant to their business. Send three small postcards or handwritten notes to your new customers, existing customers, suppliers, and so on. The cost is minimal, but the ROI can be massive. I closed a $45,000 project after sending a handwritten note to a client with an article I thought was relevant to him. I have yet to find another marketing tool that can generate a $45,000 ROI for a cost of about a dollar and about five minutes of my time. Remember, you can replace "customer" with supplier, distributor, joint venture partner, and others. All of these are valuable to creating remarkable and memorable customer experiences. For example, if you have joint venture partners where you're sharing customers via referrals, it's critical that congruence is maintained, and that expectations the referee is creating are met.

Pick-3 Example Task 3: Call Three Inactive Clients

Find three customers, suppliers, distributors, retailers, or others who have recently stopped doing business with you or haven't done business with you in a while. Call them to see how they're doing. If you don't know why they've stopped doing business with you, attempt to learn why. See what you can do to win their business back.

Pick-3 Example Task 4: Solicit Three Testimonials From Existing Clients

Call three existing customers and solicit three testimonials from them. I cover testimonials in detail in a later section. Use them everywhere. Use them to express your customer's joy to your employees and people. Use them in your preemptive Stage One marketing, and utilize them throughout the experience to emphasize the overwhelming social proof that people love your business.

Pick-3 Example Task 5: Contact Three New Clients

Pick three relatively new customers and call them to see how things are going. See if their expectations are being met. Ask them if they have any specific questions or concerns. Do what you can to address those concerns earlier rather than later.

Pick-3 Example Task 6: Create Your Own Tasks

As you can see, these are relatively simple tasks all designed to add value to the existing customer experience. You can create your own. With some of my clients, we've created dozens of simple yet powerful nurturing tasks that are completed on a daily basis. What tasks could you do on a regular basis to add more value and enrich the experience of your customers after the initial sale? That's what the Pick-3 is all about.

Track Your Results

The key thing to remember is that everyone needs to be responsible for completing these tasks on a daily basis. The reason we chose three is that doing one task three times is relatively easy. In addition, as you can see, all the tasks are incredibly simple. The main thing is that they're getting done. Our application allows for exception reporting when people are falling behind. The objective is to make sure the tasks become habitual. Think about the compound effect here: If you have 10 employees reaching out or doing three tasks a day, that's 30 customer touch points a day, and that's 900 customer touch points a month and over 10,000 a year. Now imagine that when you've got 40 employees in your office or 80, or 100. Most people can't even comprehend this much focus on retention and loyalty efforts, but there's immense power in this type of follow-up.

The tool we've provided to many of my clients is incredibly simple. Every day they log in and they're given their three tasks at random. If they truly don't love the task they've been given for the day, they can spin and request a new task. The task is laid out and there's a video, from me, describing how to complete the task as effectively as possible. They then complete the tasks, making note of what they did. If they don't complete the task, they're reminded throughout the day to get it done. And then, of course, we have exception reporting delivered to owners, managers, CEOs, and others. This is less about compliance and more about doing things to grow the business. Imagine expiring the power of compound interest when it comes to nurturing your customer base! That's what the Pick-3 is all about. Don't just claim to be the friendliest company on the planet. Don't just claim to offer a wow experience. Don't just claim the customer is number one. Back it up. This is how you do it. If you're interested in our Pick-3 tool, send me an e-mail.

Consistency Over Quantity (and Even Quality!)

Customer loyalty is about connection, and the connection is about feeling. It's the feeling my customers/readers have that I have a connection with them, and it's the feeling that they have a connection to me. Let me give you an example.

Every week I send my weekly newsletter to 30,000 subscribers. It's called *Noah's Tuesday Tidbits*.[5] Every Tuesday morning the tidbit goes out around 7 AM. And by the way, if you haven't subscribed, stop reading, head on over to NoahFleming.com, and subscribe now. I got serious about *Noah's Tuesday Tidbits* when I came to the realization that people could not only pass through Stage Two relatively quickly, but they could also spend a long time there dependent on the product, service, or need. And in many cases, even the trust building that happens in Stage Two can take months, even years. At the time of this writing, the *Tuesday Tidbit* has been delivered without fail for more than 200 weeks. Every Tuesday, it doesn't matter what's happening, that *Tidbit* is scheduled and going out. Now, here's the most important lesson to be learned: they're not always perfect. Sometimes they contain the odd typo or two, but there's consistency in it. If, and it's a big *if*, the e-mail hasn't hit the in-boxes of my subscribers by 10 AM on a Tuesday morning, I start to get e-mails from prospects and clients asking me if everything is okay, or perhaps they got unsubscribed, or can I check if the *Tidbit* went out to them. This is a sign that I've got the connection right.

One prospect in particular read the *Tidbit* for over two years. All along the trust was building, and the ideas about how I could help were being formed in his mind. He wanted to work with me but wasn't exactly sure when and how we might work together. Then, one Tuesday morning, one of the tidbits "hit him like a ton of bricks!" he said. I flew out to meet him, and we signed a $86,000 consulting engagement. Not a bad deal for me, and an excellent return on investment was generated for him. The point of this story is that consistency is almost more important that quality. I see too many businesses that don't communicate with their customers consistently enough. Guess what happens? They forget about you. I see it all the time. In Stage Four, one of the crucial lessons to be learned is the concept of familiarity. My *Tuesday Tidbit* doesn't just go out to my prospective customers, but my current and past customers too (among other things).

Too many businesses look for the one-hit wonder marketing piece. They believe they can put something out there that's instantly going to attract someone to go all of the way with them. But that's not entirely true. So what does the science tell us as it relates to Stage Four? The science tells us the more exposure someone has to your brand, the more positive they are going to feel about your brand or your company. For big businesses, this is pretty simply understood as regular and consistent branding. The more exposure we have to a brand, the more familiar we are with that brand. But I'm suggesting that almost all companies aren't consistent enough with valuable and engaging follow-up. Social psychologists have suggested that our frequent exposure to someone or something leads to a sense of familiarity. Big brands, corporations, and politicizations with deep pockets have the ability to penetrate our minds. But for nearly all companies, here's the most important part: how someone feels about your company has a lot to do with mere exposure to who you are and what you do. That's why the *Tuesday Tidbit* works, and that's why I build a strong connection with my prospects and my readers. That's why a simple newsletter can be an incredibly powerful tool for a small business. The simple fact that you're showing up every week or every month says a ton to your current and prospective customers. Most businesses aren't willing to engage in the extra work. Are you?

There's a lot of scientific evidence to suggest that the more you communicate to your audience, the more they're going to buy, the longer they're going to buy for, and the stronger relationships you'll have with your customers. Even if you do show up regularly, that doesn't mean your customers are going to buy regularly. As it relates to the recency, frequency, and monetary model, all businesses and all customers are going to have varying buying cycles. It's crucial that you understand the cycle of your business.

The Customer Iron Cage

Figure 6.2 represents the Customer Iron Cage. Unlike a typical iron cage where someone might be held against their own will, customers can't help but want to stay inside your cage. First, we offer them resistance-free selling, absent of any traditional persuasive and manipulative sales tactics. From there, we offer a remarkable customer experience in the third stage. Finally, the fourth stage is developed and continued through ongoing and consistent follow-up. See the correlation below.

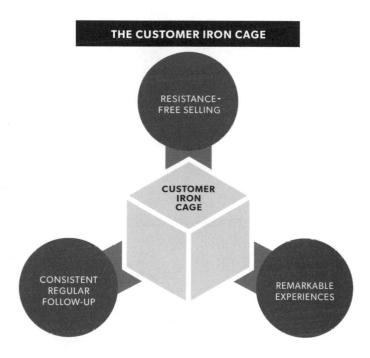

Figure 6.2: The Customer Iron Cage

The Carousel Theory

The Carousel Theory is the term I use to talk about the buying frequency of your products and services as it relates to the frequency of your communications with your customers. It indicates that all customers go through cycles. Think of the horses on a carousel moving up and down and also going around and around. Customers will have different needs, different levels of interest, and different requirements after the sale.

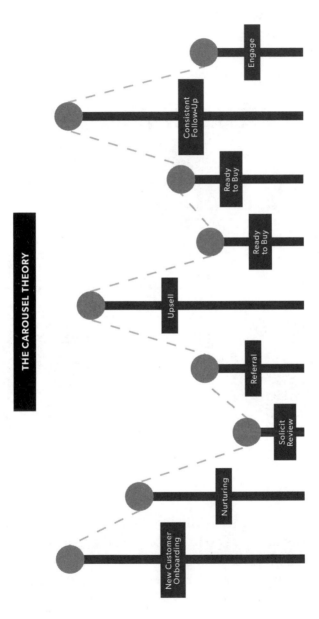

6.3 The Carousel Theory

For example, a customer may need a mattress today, and they likely won't need another one for about 10 years. They don't need one in the next three weeks, but they may buy ancillary products and services, or they refer you. They may be interested in products from your partners and learning more about improving their sleep patterns. If you're consistent in your follow-up and continue to be top of mind, then you have a better chance at getting that next big sale 10 years from now. But if you're only showing up trying to sell, then you're doing it wrong. Customers may not enter anther buying cycle for a while. That's determined by your products and services, but the Carousel Theory also suggests that it's not just buying frequency that determines your next follow-up; it's about constantly following up to build and nurture the customer relationship. Everyone loves to talk about building relationships with customers, but nobody actually explains how to do that. One way is showing up regularly and consistently as we've just discussed.

Here's the thing about the loyalty loop. If we make the assumption that the customer is only a customer up until their last transaction with us, then once they've moved into Stage Four, they're looping back to the early stages. Now, this doesn't mean that we're starting from ground zero—far from it. Assuming the initial stages were all positive, we're starting at a place of affinity. Your customers have a certain affinity to you and the previous experiences with your company. It's only a matter of time before they're back in the thick and thin of the third stage again, so everything that happens now is to continue to serve, benefit, and add value to the customer's life.

The more you communicate with your customer by adding value, which means not selling when it's not appropriate, the more trust you'll develop and the more peripheral benefits of the loop you'll experience. Do you think my *Tidbit* readers would feel the bond and connection to me if I only showed up once a month, or every other month, or even less regularly than that? Of course not, but that's what most companies are doing. They're annoying to the point of trying to consistently sell, but not add any additional value. When I talk about this with clients, I hear things like "But Noah, we're in the commercial property development industry. Why on earth would our customers and tenants be interested in hearing from us on a regular basis?" That's easy. What if you were to communicate about trends in the local economy and marketplace, new tax implications, things to look for in older buildings, case studies of proactive repairs and things you've done with other clients, and other ways for them to save money or earn more of it?

Relationship building with your clients is showing them that you care about them a bit more than just when it's time for them to open up their wallets. Your clients are begging to be acknowledged, appreciated, and perhaps most importantly, understood! The Carousel Theory suggests you work to cultivate the relationship by remaining top of mind (until it's time to buy again) but understanding that it might not be time to buy you. Yet you continue to show up, add value, build the relationship, and pitch when it's time to pitch and sell when it's time to sell. And that brings us to the most important point when it comes to caring for and nurturing your existing customer base, and that's the principle of the Appropriate Reason.

The Appropriate Reason
· ·

Many companies believe a retention strategy simply re-volves around communicating regularly and frequent-ly with their customer base, and if they do, customers will continue to buy. That couldn't be further from the truth. Consistency is more valuable than quantity, and recency and frequency are crucial underpinnings of cus-tomer retention—but the most important thing of all is the principle of the Appropriate Reason. This principle suggests that with all customer follow-up messaging and communication, there's an appropriate reason why, and an appropriate time to do it. Too many companies don't understand this, and they're reaching out with the wrong message at the wrong times. It's damaging to their abil-ity to build loyalty and develop relationships with their customers.

Communicating with your customers with the right messaging at the right time can feel like a phone call from a friend, but the wrong messaging at the wrong time is like being smacked across the face. Throughout the book, we've focused on how the customer is likely feeling at each stage of the customer experience. The post-sales ex-perience should be treated no differently. The customer is experiencing certain emotions after the sale: good, bad, or ugly. The wrong messaging at the wrong time can turn even a positive buying experience negatively. Here are a few examples.

A company I did business with delivered a pleasant experience in Stages One through Three, but they never follow up. I was quite happy they never checked in on me to see how things were going. That's not quite true.

I did finally hear from them, but it was seven months later. When they finally followed up, it was to ask me to leave a public review of my experience on a review website. This is too little and far too late. In this case, the company would likely have been better off not following up at all and instead attempting to re-engage me in the earlier stages of the cycles. It's an inappropriate request that many months later.

Salespeople, in particular, are often guilty of reaching out at the wrong time, but it's usually not their fault. They assume (and their compensation is structured based on the assumption) that once they've inked the deal, their work is done. They get their commissions, and they've moved on to find more new customers.

The care and nurturing of existing clients is someone else's problem. As I've said before, if your sales and marketing people aren't talking about what happens after the sale, then they're only doing 50 percent of their jobs.

Some companies even go so far as to have separate teams dedicated to customer loyalty or customer satisfaction, departments which rarely or never interact with the sales team. I cannot overstate how fundamentally flawed this practice is.

Repeat after me: The most important work you do is done after the first sale is made. The bulk of your efforts should be in the care and nurture of your clients.

You cannot do right by your clients if you're reaching out at inappropriate times with the wrong messaging. And please, for the love of all that is holy in this world, never ever outsource the "satisfaction" of your clients to a department without a sales responsibility.

When is the *right time*?

At the start of Stage Four, I included a quote from the CEO of Constant Contact. I included this because the very name of the company denotes Constant Contact with your customers. The more you communicate, the more you add value, the more you show up, the more likely they are to do business with you. I think Gail Goodman understands this. I want to believe she understands this. She says the single-most important thing is providing a great experience, and I have to believe she recognizes consistent communication as part of the whole experience.

Your customers want to be acknowledged and appreciated. They want to know you recognize their patronage and value it. You need to think through your Appropriate Reasons carefully and strategically. For example, is it appropriate to reach out for a testimonial the day after your product is delivered? Maybe, but maybe not. If you sell a product or service where the customer isn't likely to experience the benefits for 30, 60, or 90 days, then it doesn't make sense to ask for a testimonial a week after purchasing. But does it make sense to get in touch right away and ensure they understand the product and don't have any specific questions or need any customer service? Of course it does. That's an appropriate time with an appropriate reason. If you truly believe you're a customer-friendly, service-oriented, Zappos-like company, and you truly believe that you provide a wow experience, then you have a duty to your customers to communicate frequently and consistently.

Typically, when you get unsolicited contact from a business, the initial presumption is that they are reaching out because they want something from you. This puts most people immediately on the defensive, preparing them to be resistant to the pitch that they expect. This is not a good thing because that resistance can extend beyond this particular call or e-mail, to your brand in general. That initial resistance may be almost inevitable but the real question, once again, is how do you overcome that resistance?

If you're on a phone call, what you say immediately after your customer has answered is very important. It can either drive the customer's resistance up, or it can completely disarm it. For example, if your first words after your introduction were, "I'm delighted to tell you that you have just won $1,000 in our sweepstakes for the entry you completed when filling out your customer service evaluation!" then their resistance is likely to disappear quickly! Unfortunately, you can't do that for everyone, but is there an emotional equivalent, or at least an approximation, that can defuse resistance and increase the connection rather than fight it?

Authenticity is one of the keys to building rapport. Customers understand to a degree that a business has its goals, too. However, unless that interaction is authentic and shows the customer the benefits that might accrue to them, resistance is more likely than engagement. And that means showing the customer that your contact is for an appropriate reason.

What Is the Appropriate Reason?

One of my cardinal rules of marketing is that if you don't have anything useful and valuable to say, you're likely better off not saying it at all. Too many of us are willing to forgo the opportunity to provide immense value in hopes of simply getting out the next promotion. The goal of all communications should be to serve, add value, and enhance the lives of our customers. Frequency increases liking and familiarity, but valuable information with an appropriate reason increases trust. When I look at my *Tuesday Tidbit* readers, I can see a direct correlation between those who read most often and those who have gone on to become clients. For my private clients, I have a private newsletter and membership called *Noah's Roundtable*. The only way to get access to the roundtable is to become a client. I don't promote it, and I don't tell my prospects about this, I simply introduce it to them once we start working together. I can also find a direct correlation between those who read and watch most regularly and those I seem to have the greatest bond with.

I was in a meeting recently where one of the VPs who was quiet for most of the discussion finally chimed in. He said, "Our customers don't want to hear from us regularly! They don't want us calling or e-mailing or checking in with them. They're busy people. They only want to hear from us when they're ready to buy!" He couldn't be more wrong. Customers don't want to hear from you if it's inappropriate to contact them or at inappropriate times.

If we consider the loyalty loop, then the most appropriate type of communication begins to look a lot like what was valuable in Stage One. We continue to position ourselves as the preemptive provider and expert in our respective industries. We can do this by providing valuable, useful, educational material post-sale. We should ask for things like reviews, referrals, testimonials, and word of mouth only when the time is right. For every business, that's going to be different. For Appropriate

Reason material, ask yourself what else you can offer that adds value and enhances the lives of your customers. Here's a hint: it's always appropriate when it's not self-serving. When it's serving your interest over theirs (buy this, review this, give us this) you have to be far more discerning about right place and the right time.

Can You Really Love Your Customers?

There have been a lot of books over the past couple of years that talk about the concepts of "loving your customers" and "hugging your customers." I've read dozens of them. The major problem I have with most of them is the focus on solving customer-related issues after they happen. They're reactive in nature, and almost all major business improvements I've been involved with happen when we're proactive in our efforts. With the loyalty loop, we've taken a far more holistic view of the customer experience from start to finish. In the final stage, the key to the customer's mind is quite simple. You owe it to your customers to communicate frequently, not just when it's time for them to buy. You owe it to them to continuously add new value and show them that you care about them. And if you don't do this, then you're doing your customers a major disservice. Most of the loop is about staying top of mind and in the customer's mind. It's got very little to do with the tactics of influence and more to do with just understanding what the customer is feeling at each stage of buying experience, and how you can make the experience as positive as possible.

Treat Customers Like Members

Many companies make decisions about their clients based on total revenue spent. They take their top 10–20 percent of best spenders and work to surprise, delight, and care for those customers. There are times when this works and times when it doesn't. Consider, for example, Bill Gates' party at your fictional nightclub last night. Bill had all the ladies swooning over him and dropped $100,000 on incredible bottle service. Bottles of Remy Martin Louis XIII Cognac were flowing at $6,000 a bottle. This morning, he's your best and most valuable customer. Regardless of how he got to your club, the likelihood of him coming back again, and again, and again, are pretty much next to none. I'm sure Bill loves to party, but this is the fallacy of using total revenue spend to determine your "best customers." Contrast that now to the 836 25- to 35-year-old guys who come in on a weekly basis dropping $600 to $800 like clockwork. They are your best customers, but using total revenue, they're likely to be missed. You're focusing on the wrong customers and it's costing you money. Bill Gates is not your best customer. You can't always focus on the individual customers. Look to understand what groups of customers you have that are preferred in terms of current value, future business, and referral potential. You need to understand who your best customers are and make offers that are exclusive to them.

My good friend Robbie Baxter released a wonderful book in 2015 called *The Membership Economy: Find Your Super Users, Master the Forever Transaction, and Build Recurring Revenue*. In the book, she shares various examples of businesses using the membership model to grow and retain customers. The membership model is one of the most powerful tools you can consider in the loyalty loop. If your customers can benefit by doing business with you on a regular, ongoing basis, then it makes sense to offer them that solution. Very few businesses think this way, but Robbie offers dozens of less traditional examples of businesses embracing the model. For example, I can make a strong case that if customers love a restaurant, then offering them a membership with a repeat monthly purchase can make a lot of sense. We can influence the loyalty loop by delivering a remarkable and memorable customer experience that appeals to the mind of our customer, but if your buying cycle and frequency is rather short, think about all the ways you can offer customers a longer-term commitment.

Action Step: The Preferred Customer Club

Schedule a special event, or even periodic events, to reward, acknowledge, and show your existing customers you appreciate them. Last year I had my first-ever Evergreen Summit. I invited half a dozen of my top clients to dinner the night before in one of the best restaurants in Canada.

Create new levels of loyalty for your best and move valuable customers. Most loyalty programs are terrible ineffective. They give perks and rewards once a certain threshold of spending is met. I suggest doing it a little bit different by adding additional value in other ways. Look for ways to offer your best customers unique advantages like early access to new products or higher levels of support (the Bat Phone: 24/7 support line). Consider preferential pricing or bonuses based on a certain spend.

Brainstorm all the little extras you can do for your preferred customers after the sale in Stage Four. Don't forget that they look back around. Brainstorm all the little extras you can do for your preferred customers on subsequent purchases and transactions with your company.

Brainstorm all the ways you could embrace the membership economy and create long-term offerings for your customers. Think about things like ongoing product deliveries, extended service, additional support, and so on.

Spiraling the Loyalty Loop

The core philosophy of this book is pretty simple. Instead of spending the bulk of your time, energy, and resources in new customer acquisition, you should invest heavily in ensuring you're doing whatever you can to deliver an amazing, remarkable, and most important of all, memorable customer experience. If you want to grow your business, increase your competitive advantage, and create dramatic profit returns, then the Customer Loyalty Loop is one way to do it.

The loyalty loop is about providing value throughout the entire customer experience and recognizing the entire customer experience encompasses the whole experience from the first time the prospect hears about your business, to happily ever after. Let me share a brief story with you, a true story, but one that offers us a perfect parable to close out the book.

The Loop in Action

Last year, I needed to get some work done at my house. I needed a general contractor, so I decided to look online to see who was local and who might be able to help. I visited many of their websites, filled out contact forms, and called a few of them. Out of the 10 I called, only one got back to me promptly. At least four still haven't gotten back to me at the time of this writing months ago; five more were confusing and instantly tried to get me to commit to things before even coming out to see me. They wanted to quote pricing without seeing the work or even asking enough questions to understand what I truly needed. Only one of them offered to come out and review exactly what I needed. He was incredible. There were some things he nailed.

First, when I reached out to him, he got back to me quickly. It was within 90 minutes. We had a friendly chat, and he said something that got my attention. He said, "You know; there are a lot of great contractors in town; I know them all, and I'm sure any of us would do a great job! But because of what you've explained you need to have done, here are the six things you need to watch out for...." He went on to explain six things that I was going to need to look for in my job. He wasn't badmouthing his competition. He was providing value. Preemptively, he created a story and told it to me in a way that was vivid and fascinating. That's Stage One of the Customer Loyalty Loop.

A day or two later, he showed up and walked me through all of the options. He was just how I expected him to be. He was clean cut, drove a nice clean truck with his company's logo on it, and he was well dressed. He took his time to help me understand everything that was wrong. He explained the options I had available, and which would be the best value. He showed me the cheapest options and the more expensive options. He took his time to explain each one. He also reaffirmed everything we had discussed on the phone in regard to what to watch out for. Finally, he took the time to listen to my concerns and answer my questions. Needless to say, he removed all the resistance from the conversion process. That's Stage Two of the Customer Loyalty Loop.

When the day came to do the work, his people showed up in a similar truck. They were clean cut, professional, and courteous. When they arrived, one rang our doorbell to let us know they were about to start working. It was early morning, and my kids were just waking up. They wanted to let us know that we might hear some equipment, but overall it wouldn't be that loud. A couple of hours later, my children were playing in our driveway while the guys did the work. They didn't litter my lawn with cigarette butts, use inappropriate language, or listen to loud music. Instead, they did the job, and they did it well! My kids got a kick out of watching them enjoy their lunch break. A couple of times throughout the day, they showed me how things were progressing. I was impressed! About half way through the day, the owner whom I had I talked to earlier arrived to inspect his team's progress. I saw him talking to the guys and looking at a few things. He called me over and pointed out a few additional repairs that I should have done. Was I being upsold? No. In fact, he said he couldn't do the work himself, but he could recommend a few people in town that could do it. He then explained if I used any of the people he suggested, that he would get a referral bonus from them, and I would get his discount. He assured me the work would be top-notch, and he would only recommend people he knew could do the job well because his reputation was on the line. To me, this was truly a Remarkable Moment! Never before had I been treated by a contractor like this.

He left, and then returned at the end of the day to inspect the work. Needless to say, they did a fantastic job. When I asked if I could write him a check right then and there, he stated that they would invoice me, and there was no rush. The invoice came days later with a handwritten note from the contractor telling me to contact him directly if I had any issues. That's Stage Three of the Customer Loyalty Loop.

Months went on, and my life returned to normal. During that time, I think I had referred the contractor at least a dozen times to people who needed various jobs done. About three months later, my daughter said, "Daddy, someone is here!" I looked outside to see the contractor inspecting that old repair. I went out and said hello. He was friendly and stated that he just wanted to stop by and personally thank me for the referrals I had sent him. He said he was just checking in to ensure the work they did was holding up. It was. And then, he asked if I'd be willing to provide a testimonial he could use on their website. Of course, I happily gave the referral. And there you have Stage Four of the Customer Loyalty Loop.

This contractor provided a customer experience that was leaps and bounds above what I've seen and witnessed with my own eyes in multi-million and even billion-dollar companies. The best part of all? He had developed it himself, and most importantly, he *stuck to it* every single time. He understood each stage of the Customer Loyalty Loop and treated each part of the customer experience with a level of gravitas and respect leaps and bounds beyond any of his competitors.

During the past 10 years, I've worked with some incredibly talented people, in some extremely successful companies, but I've had to fight tooth and nail to implement even *some* of the ideas in this book into their businesses. But when we do get them to execute even a fraction of what's required, the results are always dramatic and they're always grateful that they finally relented and listened.

Big companies often get stuck in internal politicking, inability to challenge some departments, or paralysis by analysis in that they don't know how to look objectively at the entire customer experience, from initial contact to happily ever after. Now there's no excuse.

Your company might be big, or your business might be small. That doesn't matter. What is important is that this short story serves as a great reminder to all of us that whether you're a giant or a one-man show, the basic structure of successful sales and marketing is all the same. If you can get the customer experience right, you win. And you'll win every single time.

So let's end right here with one simple question: How does your customer's experience match up to my local contractor's? Is it as good as his? If not, we should talk.

Notes

Introduction

1. Noah Fleming, *Cultivate the Enduring Customer Loyalty That Keeps Your Business Thriving* (New York: Amacom, 2015).
2. Jenny Beightol, "Small Business Survey 2016: Marketing & Customer Retention Trends," *Belly*, May 10, 2016, *www.bellycard.com/resources/customer-retention-marketing-insights*.
3. Robert Cialdini, *Influence: The Psychology of Persuasion* (New York: Collins, 2007).

1. The Science of Experience

1. Daniel Kahneman, *Thinking, Fast and Slow* (New York: Farrar, Straus, and Giroux, 2013).
2. Leon Festinger, *A Theory of Cognitive Dissonance* (Stanford, Calif. : Stanford University Press, 1957).

3. Check out Elizabeth Loftus's fantastic Ted Talk, *How Reliable Is Your Memory?*, *www.ted.com/ talks/elizabeth_loftus_the_fiction_of_memory.*

4. Daniel Simons, Counter-Intuition, *www.youtube.com/watch?v=eb4TM19DYDY.*

5. Melanie Tannenbaum, "Are Your 9/11 Memories Really Your Own?", *Scientific American,* September 11, 2013, *http:// blogs.scientificamerican.com/psysociety/ are-your-911-memories-really-your-own/.*

6. *Business News Daily,* "Relaxed Shoppers Spend More Money," *www.businessnewsdaily.com/1269-relaxed-shoppers-spend-more.html*

7. Sheena Iyengar, *The Art of Choosing* (New York: Hatchette Book Group, 2010).

3. Stage One: Imagination Before Persuasion

1. Julian Watkins, *The 100 Greatest Advertisements 1852–1958: Who Wrote Them and What They Did* (New York: Dover Publications, 2012).

2. Want to try and win the $100 bounty? Check out the hunt here: *www.antarctic-circle.org/advert. htm.*

3. *https://en.wikipedia.org/wiki/Scientific_Advertising*

4. Jay Abraham has fantastic tactical marketing materials on the power of preeminent marketing. Check out all of Jay's material, but start with *Getting Everything You Can Out of All You've Got*: *https://amzn.com/0312284543*

5. Ad Age and Schlitz Brewing purity claims: http://adage.com/article/adage-encyclopedia/ schlitz-brewing/98868/

6. Dan Gilbert, *Stumbling on Happiness* (New York: Vintage Books, 2007).

7. A collection of fascinating social experiments can be found in the book *Experiments With People: Revelations From Social Psychology* by Robert P. Abelson, Kurt P. Frey, and Aiden P. Gregg (New York: Psychology Press, 2012).

4. Stage Two: Conversion Not Coercion

1. Check out *Evergreen* and my blog to understand the concept of the Messy Closet Theory. The theory suggests that organization is often far more desirable than a messy, confusing closet. This concept applies to your storefront, your website, your phone systems, and so on. *http://noahfleming.com/the-messy-closet-theory-customer-experience/*

2. In *Glengarry Glen Ross*, Alec Baldwin's character delivers one of the most fantastic monologues ever. View it here: *www.youtube.com/watch?v=Q4PE2hSqVnk*

3. "Jets bringing their own toilet paper to London because 'why not?'," by Zac Jackson, NBCSports, October 1, 2015, *http://profootballtalk.nbcsports.com/2015/10/01/jets-bringing-their-own-to-toilet-paper-to-london-because-why-not/.*

4. Erik Knowles, "Resistance and Persuasion," *www.drknowles.com/resistancepersuasion.html*

5. Jay Haley, Uncommon Therapy: The Psychiatric Techniques of Milton H. Erickson (New York: W. W. Norton, 1993).

5. Stage Three: Experience Choreography

1. John M. Darley and Daniel C. Batson, "'From Jerusalem to Jericho': A Study of Situational and Dispositional Variables in Helping Behavior,"

Journal of Personality and Social Psychology 27 (July 1973).

2. Martin E. P. Seligman, "Learned Helplessness," *Annual Review of Medicine* 23 (February 1973), 401–412.

3. Chris Hurn, "Stuffed Giraffe Shows What Customer Service Is All About," *The Huffington Post*, updated July 17, 2012. This is the story used by every customer service speaker on the planet: *www.huffingtonpost.com/chris-hurn/stuffed-giraffe-shows-wha_b_1524038.html*.

4. Lindsey Rupp, "Delight the Customer or Lose Your Job: Restoration Hardware CEO Sends Scorching Memo." Bloomberg, February 25, 2016.

5. See the e-mail sent to Donald Trump's e-mail database about using his helicopter in Scotland: *http://noahfleming.com/how-to-borrow-donald-trumps-helicopter/*.

6. Andrea Petersen, "How Luxury Hotels Decide If You Deserve a Perk," *The Wall Street Journal*, April 29, 2015, *www.wsj.com/articles/how-luxury-hotels-decide-if-you-deserve-a-perk-1430333168*.

7. Martin Lindstrom, *Buyology: Truth and Lies About Why We Buy* (New York: Broadway Books, 2010).

8. Casper.com, the best mattress ever.

9. Ikea employees share information on the "Open the Wallet" sections of the store. *http://mentalfloss.com/article/73388/19-behind-scenes-secrets-ikea-employees*

10. Antonio Damasio, *Descartes' Error: Emotion, Reason and the Human Brain* (New York: Penguin, 2005).

6. Stage Four: Happily Ever After

1. Gail Goodman, "How Gail Goodman Built Constant Contact's Funnel to Build the $1 Billion Email Marketing Empire," *Kissmetrics Blog*: *https://blog.kissmetrics.com/gail-goodman-funnel-optimization/*.

2. The Serial Position Effect, *https://en.wikipedia.org/wiki/Serial_position_effect*.

3. Learn more about NPS at *http://NetPromoter.com*.

4. Jennifer Kaplan, "The Inventor of Customer Satisfaction Surveys Is Sick of Them, Too," Bloomberg Technology, May 4, 2016, *www.bloomberg.com/news/articles/2016-05-04/tasty-taco-helpful-hygienist-are-all-those-surveys-of-any-use*.

5. Sign up for my *Tuesday Tidbit* at *http://NoahFleming.com*.

Index